Eli Whitney
and the
Birth of
American Technology

Constance McL. Green

Eli Whitney

and the

Birth of American

Technology

Edited by Oscar Handlin

 LONGMAN

An imprint of Addison Wesley Longman, Inc.

New York • Reading, Massachusetts • Menlo Park, California • Harlow, England
Don Mills, Ontario • Sydney • Mexico City • Madrid • Amsterdam

LIBRARY OF CONGRESS CATALOG CARD NO. 56-5930

00 01 02   09 08 07

ISBN 0-673-39338-0

Editor's Preface

THE AMERICANS who had won political independence from Great Britain in 1776 were determined from the start also to attain economic independence. They wished to stand on their own feet. They wished also to prove the correctness of their acts of resistance. The material prosperity of the new nation was to vindicate the Revolution; freed from the shackling imperial restraints, the New World would far outdistance the achievements of the Old.

The struggle to develop the productive system called attention to the importance of manufacturing. For decades, the Americans sought means to stimulate the industry that would assure their economic independence.

For a long time these ambitions were frustrated. Manufacturing was slow to grow in the United States, for it faced enormous social obstacles. The nation had, after all, not yet passed out of its frontier condition, and labor of any kind was expensive, while skilled labor was often quite inaccessible.

The founding fathers were optimists. But they had only to compare their own situation with that of the European countries to perceive the difficulties in the way of rapid industrialization. The new factories that appeared with growing frequency in England and on the Continent were manned by an industrial proletariat that had no counterpart in the United States. And the traditional workshops that had already brought industrial wealth to the Old World depended upon the skills of numerous artisans, such as did not exist on this side of the ocean. From this point of view, the prospect for the quick development of American industry was slim indeed.

As the nineteenth century began, however, these deficiencies were already producing their own remedy. The lack of hands and the shortage of traditional skills made Americans alert to the necessity of finding other means of getting their jobs done. On the farms and in the urban shops, men fell into the practice of seeking devices to save labor. The inability to rely upon habit compelled Americans to tinker, to look at the processes of production from fresh points of view, to contrive ways of sparing labor. That compulsion would be immensely significant for the future of American technology.

This was the background against which Eli Whitney came to maturity. His own life and ambitions were cast in quite another mold at first; but a series of specific challenges led him to exercise his ingenuity in technology and made him an engineer. His cotton gin revolutionzed Southern agriculture. And the problems of manufacturing large quantities of guns drove him to develop principles important in his own time, and even more important later. The application of those principles would one day give American industry the structure within which it more than fulfilled the ambitions of the Revolutionary generation.

This is the absorbing story Constance Green has told through a skillful mingling of personal narrative and technologica. analysis.

OSCAR HANDLIN

Contents

Eli Whitney
and the
Birth of
American Technology

To my Grandchildren
Alice Angell Green and Andrew Reynolds Clark

Whose lives, like those of their forebears,
are affected by the work of Eli Whitney

I

Economic Problems of the United States at the End of the Revolution

ELI WHITNEY grew up in a world preoccupied with the problems created by national independence. Americans had fought the Revolution partly to assert their rights as free men, partly to enjoy the boundless prosperity they believed must follow upon independence and peace. Expectations had run high that the United States would become a great economic power as soon as the war was won; a rapidly expanding commerce would benefit the entire nation and justify the Revolution itself.

Peace had been disillusioning; it neither brought prosperity nor restored the material well-being the colonies had known. The building of a nation in the face of that disillusionment was the work of many men. Political leaders drafted the plan; men in all walks of life sought to carry it out. Good will, unfortunately, was not enough for the task. It required also the development of a new economic system grounded in native resources. The abundance of rich well-watered land within the United States, the forests to furnish lumber and fuel, the bogs containing iron, the still undiscovered mineral deposits and the tumbling streams to supply water power were potential sources of wealth, but to exploit them the country needed men. Herein lay a difficulty. The population was small and thinly spread over the nation's territory; hundreds of miles contained no white settlers at all. Because the United States in 1790 had scarcely 4,600,000 inhabitants, the new order Americans hoped to build must rely less upon man power than upon novel methods of production. By providing tools essential to this change Eli Whitney performed a vital service to his country.

The war had been costly. Despite the fertility of the land, in the 1780's the country was impoverished. The productivity of long neglected farms had declined sharply. Americans still depended upon Europe for most manufactured goods and upon foreign trade to supply the means of paying for imports. Merchants who had resented the restrictions imposed by the mother country now learned that as colonists they had also benefited from commercial privileges denied citizens of an independent nation.

Intelligent, well-informed Americans perceived the problem: if the new states were to regain the prosperity of colonial days, they must either find commodities for export which the outside world wanted, or scrape up hard money, or develop a carrying trade that foreign governments would tolerate, or make the United States self-sufficient. Overwhelming obstacles seemingly closed off each course. Complete self-sufficiency was patently impossible for a people who aspired to the role of a great power. With the English Navy patrolling the seas to enforce the

British Navigation Laws, the profits of the American carrying trade were steadily shrinking. Prospects of improvement were slim as long as Parliament endorsed the views Lord Sheffield had expressed in *Observations on the Commerce of the American States with Europe and the West Indies*, which argued against generosity to a people who had voluntarily withdrawn from the British Empire. Although American ships barred from the British sugar islands could enter French, Dutch and Danish ports in the Caribbean, and even some of the Spanish, the money-making "long haul" thence direct to Europe was closed to vessels flying the flag of the United States; continental nations, like Britain, reserved this trade for themselves. Bullion, scarce throughout the colonial period in this part of the New World, was now even harder to obtain. Circumstances beyond American control thus narrowed the choice to development of export staples.

To find staple articles for export was itself a problem, for the United States must sell goods European nations would accept, and parts of the country were ill-suited to producing the type of commodity wanted. New England, in particular, had little to offer Europe. The cod and haddock caught on the Newfoundland banks could not support unaided a flourishing foreign trade, and agricultural surpluses were meager. Beside the fisheries and her carrying trade, the vessels built in her shipyards, forest products, and the molasses, loaf sugar and rum made from West Indian raw sugar had formed the basis of New England's earlier prosperity. The dislocation of commerce at the end of the war therefore caused acute suffering. After 1785 successful voyages to the Far East brought wealth to merchants who dared tie up capital for two or three years, and in 1792 the outbreak of war between Britain and France enabled shipmasters of lesser means to recapture much of their former carrying trade and thereby reopen markets for all New England products. But that still left the economy of the region on a precarious basis.

Meanwhile, although the fertile fields of the Middle States were again producing the cattle and the grain that in pre-Revolutionary days had given the "Bread Colonies" their name, here too the closing of the British West Indian ports to Americans brought hardship to merchants and to the farmers who supplied them. Foodstuffs marketable abroad only in seasons of foreign crop failures scarcely ranked as export "staples." As in New England, only the merchant princes of the East Indian and China trade prospered. In and about Philadelphia the skilled artisans whose carpets, glassware and ironwork, and whose experiments with spinning and weaving woolen, flax and a little cotton had made the neighborhood the center of such manufacturing as the United States had, were in turn handicapped by the widespread poverty that obliged potential consumers at home to forgo purchases.

Matters were worse in the South. Fiercely fought battles and never-ending guerrilla warfare during the Revolution had devastated the countryside. Whole towns had disappeared. As the enemy had killed or carried off slaves, the elaborate dyking of plantation rice fields in the tidal marshlands of Georgia and South Carolina had suffered irreparable neglect. The rice crop of 1783 was less than half that of an average prewar year; and the culture of that staple never regained its one-time importance. Furthermore, South Carolina and Georgia had abandoned the cultivation of indigo when British bounties ceased to support it, and at the end of the Revolution the cheapness of East Indian indigo had prevented revival of the American enterprise. Tobacco, the great staple of much of the South, not only had exhausted the soil of the older tidewater plantations but, because of oversupply, was no longer profitable. While corn crops, hogs and potatoes staved off starvation, planters saddled with slaves to feed searched vainly for a money-making crop. Most of the upland was wilderness, and, even near the seaboard, large plantations included hundreds ot acres still untilled. The value of slaves dropped steadily, for who would benefit from putting them to raise crops neither Europe nor America wanted or knew how to use? "The staple of America at present consists of land," observed an English traveler in the South. And uncultivated land, whatever its promise, brought no immediate returns.

Lack of easy communication between one region and another added to the agricultural distress of the South and the commercial depression of the North. Ratification of the Constitution created a formal political unity, but the United States remained cut apart into states separated by distance and want of transportation. Ignorance in one area about the needs of another prevented co-operation. Newspapers were few, and their distribution was limited. Long after the establishment of a Federal postal service, a letter posted in Maine was twenty days in reaching Georgia, and the cost of using the mails deterred correspondence. Men in remote places in those days before postage stamps were known to accept postmasterships in order to avoid the high fee for every letter they wrote to relatives or friends. All transport was expensive, slow, and uncertain. Coastwise vessels were small and uncomfortable, their freight capacity 250 tons or less, and voyages around Cape Hatteras were as hazardous in the late eighteenth century as in the sixteenth. In the more protected waters of Chesapeake Bay and Long Island Sound, shipping, though safer, was irregular; vessels sailed from New York for Europe more frequently than for Providence, Rhode Island. River boats, the easiest means of shipping goods inland, also were slow and expensive. Cartage overland was slower still and costlier.

Travel was a serious undertaking. People moving more than a short distance from home faced not only expense but acute discomfort and, at times, danger. Every journey was time-consuming. Stagecoaches ran between Boston and New York two or three times a week, and between New York and Philadelphia rather oftener. But the stage from Boston to Manhattan took four days in good summer weather, seven in winter, and nine or ten in snowstorms; the trip on to Philadelphia took at best another two days. Although a fairly good road lay between Philadelphia and Baltimore, the traveler had to cross the broad expanse of the Susquehanna in an open boat. Farther south roads in the interior were little more than tracks; in the Tidewater, rivers and creeks did duty for highways.

Travel by stagecoach cost about six cents a mile, and the charges at inns for food and shelter added at least two dollars and fifty cents every twenty-four hours. Few people could afford to pay such prices. As late as 1800, men carrying the United States mail south of Virginia went on horseback, and Jefferson noted that to reach Washington from Monticello he had to cross eight rivers, five of them without either bridges or ferries. "The same bad roads and difficult rivers, connecting the same small towns," wrote Henry Adams, "stretched into the same forests in 1800 as when the armies of Braddock and Amherst pierced the western and northern wilderness, except that these roads extended a few miles farther from the seacoast. Nature was rather man's master than his servant, and the five million Americans struggling with the untamed continent seemed hardly more competent to their task than the beavers and buffalo who had for countless generations made bridges and roads of their own."

The inroads of disease also heightened Americans' anxieties and discontents during the first years of independence and peace. People the world over, it is true, suffered from ailments no one could diagnose, let alone cure, but in the United States the frequent recurrence of illness gave a peculiarly somber tone to economic troubles. Smallpox, yellow fever, tuberculosis, heart trouble, dysentery, malaria, scarlet fever, diphtheria, measles, rheumatic fever, "biliousness," kidney infections — these and a host of other maladies, their symptoms described too inaccurately to identify, took constant toll. Virtually every personal letter, whoever its author, discussed the writer's health, and not as a mere formality, but as a matter of deep concern. Year after year scores of women died in childbirth, and the rows of miniature headstones in any ancient cemetery attested to the number of children who died young. The population consequently increased slowly. In eighteenth-century America, illness sapped men's vitality, hampered their work and shortened their lives. For a young nation to whose growth every productive citizen was important this constant drain on her man power was disastrous.

Men accepted illness and early death as the will of God, but Americans firmly believed that in other respects they themselves could better their lot. Ideas differed about how to proceed. Some men thought the path lay in political action, some in promoting domestic manufactures, others in fostering new agricultural products, and a few in pursuing several courses at once. Each plan had some justification.

Daniel Shays and his adherents among the debt-ridden farmers of western Massachusetts believed a new revolution could best cure their ills. Armed force alone, they contended, would induce the moneyed aristocrats to agree to a more equitable distribution of power and wealth, for just as more than one Massachusetts merchant had supported the Revolution in hopes of improving trade, so humbler men had fought to achieve a more democratic social order. Both groups had suffered disappointment, but poverty-stricken farmers burdened with taxes regarded the politically influential merchant class as responsible for the back country's troubles. Shays had no complete program in mind; his plan was to obtain for his followers a larger voice in the state's counsels and thereby lower taxes and halt foreclosure of mortgages. Shays's Rebellion failed. But in other parts of the country men examining the persisting social disparities continued to look to political changes to transform want into plenty. In 1787, opponents of ratification of the Constitution included not only representatives who feared the sacrifice of states' rights but politically inexperienced persons who considered the closer union proposed but a new weapon in the hands of the rich to keep lesser people from helping themselves.

On the other hand, Alexander Hamilton, Tench Coxe of Pennsylvania, and converts to their views, while recognizing the need of a stronger union, saw in the growth of American manufactures the means of lessening the economic strains upon the new nation. Material want, not suffrage restrictions and political inequalities, created unrest and threatened the United States' future. Manufacturing, its proponents reasoned, would provide employment for women and children lacking other gainful work, and, more important, freedom from dependence upon European manufactures would permit the country to keep its hard money at home to use for further constructive investment. Though the difficulties were great, the rewards would be greater. Most Americans of the post-Revolutionary era, however, put scant faith in the scheme. In their eyes the want of ready capital, the shortage of skilled labor and the lack of power-driven machinery in the United States must long delay, perhaps forever prevent, the rise of manufacturing industries here.

Clearly the most feasible and quickest way out of the national dilemma was to develop a staple product to supplement the meager exports of tobacco and turpentine, dried fish and pipe staves, breadstuffs and salt beef. The commodity must be something Europe needed in quantity and which the United States could supply more readily than could foreign powers and their colonies. And because Americans were learning the soundness of Lord Sheffield's prophecy that they would continue to seek English markets — where, despite duties, the superior service at British ports, familiar weights and measures and a common language offered irresistible advantages — the article should be something for which English demand was insistent and mounting. What American commodity that could be was a moot question in the mid-1780's. A decade later men knew the answer: cotton.

In 1785, the green-seed "upland" variety of cotton, destined shortly thereafter to become the mainstay of the United States export trade, was virtually unknown as a commercial article. J. D. B. DeBow, that authority on the commerce of the antebellum South, declared in 1852 that South Carolina planters had shipped seven bags to England in 1748, another small lot in 1754, and ten bags more in 1770; but before 1790 cotton was still an experimental crop. From Virginia southward, farmers had for years raised a little to spin and weave into homespun for their own households, and the gleaming white flowers gave the plants a place in Southern gardens. The provincial assemblies of South Carolina and Virginia in 1775 had urged the wisdom of cotton cultivation; that year Alexander Hamilton had hopefully predicted that the Southern colonies might "with due cultivation in a couple of years" produce "enough to clothe the whole continent." Farmers did not respond. In 1784 eight bags of cotton shipped from Charleston to Liverpool occasioned protests from customs officials, who at first refused to believe that the United States could raise so much. Yet in the next twenty years cotton completely altered the economic status of the nation.

The increasing importance of American cotton was due to the phenomenal growth of the British cotton textile industry. Before the 1780's, wool and flax had been the chief staples for clothing in the Western world. Only the very wealthy could afford the fine cotton muslins and calicoes imported from India. In England, cotton spinning and weaving, begun in Manchester in the reign of Charles I, was still at the accession of George III a minor industry. Yet because it was new, tradition, perpetuated by the guilds and other vested interests, had not intervened to dictate its processing. Producers in Lancashire seized upon innovations ignored by the older trades. John Kay's flying shuttle, patented in 1733, John Wyatt's roller spinning machine of 1738, James Hargreaves's spinning jenny, perfected twenty-five years later, then Arkwright's water frame of 1769, and in 1779 Samuel Crompton's mule, never patented at all, combined to bring about an industrial revolution in the production of cotton cloth. Upon the expiration of Arkwright's patent in 1785, cotton factories equipped with his spinning frames sprang up throughout Lancashire, and the demand for raw cotton was soon outrunning supply. British eagerness to obtain the staple was the United States' opportunity.

The effects of the British inventions for cotton manufacture were compounded, moreover, by another line of innovations that altered the nature of English industrial power. At the opening of the seventeenth century, the shift to coal from wood necessitated by the depletion of English forests had set a basic transformation in motion. A long succession of mechanical developments deriving from the inspiration of Newton's *Principia* reached important milestones — first in Thomas Newcomen's steam pump, then in 1777 in Watt and Boulton's commercially successful steam engine. The steam engine, and the precision tools that permitted its building, multiplied the consequences of the revolution in cotton manufacture. Before 1800, steam was supplying power to cotton mills. In the west of England, factories — their labor force composed largely of women and small children — were displacing the households where man and wife spun and wove at home.

These swift technological changes affected the United States profoundly and quickly. The new machines insatiably gobbling up raw cotton created the commercial opening the United States sought. Cotton from the West Indies, Brazil, Smyrna and India no longer sufficed. Although the slowness of communication between the Old World and the New and within the United States delayed realization in

America of what these changes could mean, Tench Coxe saw the opportunity and advocated pursuing it as early as 1786. Having attended the Annapolis Convention, called to discuss a trade agreement among the Middle States, he was keenly aware of the country's needs, and, as he told the story later, when he observed a cotton plant growing in an Annapolis garden, he concluded that cotton would provide the hoped-for answer.

The idea was not immediately convincing. Cotton growing, Coxe argued, would revive Southern agriculture by providing a commodity for export with a sure market in Europe. Cotton raising, moreover, would nurture American industry by furnishing manufactures at home with a "redundant staple" — in the twentieth century a truly meaningful phrase. Coxe evidently assumed that skilled workmen in the United States could build spinning machines as good as the English or that American enterprisers could evade the Parliamentary prohibition on the export of British machinery, as they had before the Revolution. In 1775 a Philadelphia company had installed a twenty-four-spindle jenny, only to have the British confiscate it when they captured the city. The stumbling block to Coxe's plan, initially, lay in the doubts of Southerners about the utility of attempting to raise upland cotton commercially. The plant grew almost as a weed in many places; but planters had learned from experience in setting their slaves to prepare the short-staple variety for spinning and weaving cloth for household use that the task of stripping the tenacious green seeds from the fiber was extremely time-consuming. As a slave could clean but a pound a day, the marketable quantities were small, and the money return was negligible.

In one small section of the South, hope rose in 1786 when a planter on one of the low-lying sandy islands off the coast of Georgia produced a little cotton of a variety new to the United States — silky, long-fibered and, most important of all, easily stripped of its black seeds. Two years later a bag of Sea Island cotton brought a handsome price in London. Two or three other planters on Sapelo and St. Simon islands had similar success, and by 1789 some twenty plantations on the islands were growing this promising variety. At last, Southerners thought, a solution to their problems lay in sight. Grow black-seed cotton inland, and every plantation and farm in the region would profit.

How to get the seed at first seemed the only question. Southern loyalists, re-established by the Crown in the Bahamas after the Revolution, had presented the first lots of seed to friends in Georgia; Frank Levett, Colonel Roger Kelsal and other planters on the coastal islands hoarded their supply. Then the South discovered that the problem was more serious. When plantation owners inland at length succeeded in getting seed to try, the experiments were a failure. Long-staple cotton would not grow in the interior.

By 1790, however, the stakes had·become too high to allow Southerners to abandon their efforts. That year, as encouragement to planters, a duty of three cents a pound on raw cotton imported from the West Indies and Brazil went into effect in the United States. Alexander Hamilton's fa·

mous *Report on Manufactures* in 1791 told of the success of the "Manufactory at Providence" where Samuel Slater, secretly emigrated from England, had built from memory machines like the carefully guarded ones in Arkwright and Strutt's factory in Derby. News of that launching of an American cotton textile industry added incentive for cotton growers. Were more needed, it came from the published statistics on Great Britain's increased imports of raw cotton: in 1783 some 9,000,000 pounds; in 1790 over 28,000,000 pounds. By 1792, how to cross Sea Island with upland cotton, or else how to strip the green seeds efficiently from the short-staple variety, had become topics of constant debate in the South. The first proposal — development of a hybrid that would combine the "baldheaded" black seeds of Sea Island with the hardiness of upland cotton — seemed feasible. Indeed, some evidence suggested that the cotton shipped from seaboard plantations during the colonial era had been a short-staple, black-seed species. Unhappily, years of experimenting proved the impossibility of growing it inland. Conditions of climate and soil, not the seed itself, permitted the black-seed variety to flourish in the islands, and in a narrow stretch of mainland between Charleston, South Carolina, and Florida, and nowhere else in the United States. The second possibility — making green-seed cotton marketable — seemed less promising to Southerners in the early 1790's.

Escape from the dilemma with which the United States had struggled for more than a decade was at last in sight. Only cotton seeds stood between the nation and economic recovery. Clean cotton was an ideal staple to promote a

mounting prosperity. The South would profit from gr
ing the crop, the North from transporting it to Europe
manufacturing cloth at home. Cotton exports would part
redeem America's unfavorable balance of trade and enabl
men to accumulate capital. Capital invested in new ventures or more cotton fields would help develop the country. As material well-being spread, health might improve;
men might live longer and the man-power shortage accord-
ingly shrink.

Eli Whitney's genius first solved the problem of the
Southern agrarian, and slightly later mapped the path for
the Northern enterpriser unwilling to depend upon favorable commercial policies of foreign governments. Whitney's cotton gin transformed the South, and his introduction of novel industrial techniques led the North gradually
to revise old habits, to find in precision machines a partial
substitute for man power and in manufacturing a supplement to foreign trade.

I I

Yankee Youth

ELI WHITNEY was born in Westborough, Massachusetts, on December 8, 1765. His father, for whom young Eli was named, came from a family of respectable farmers; his mother, Elizabeth Fay, from the substantial yeomanry of Massachusetts. The family was middle-class. By the standards of the day Eli Whitney, Senior, steeped as he was in the New England tradition of "uniform industry and strict frugality," provided well for his children — Eli, Elizabeth, Benjamin and Josiah. His wife, worn by bearing four children within five years and by the numberless tasks of the eighteenth-century farm household, became an invalid after Josiah's birth. Much of the seven and a half years of her illness she lay bedridden. Long afterward, her daughter remarked that the children "were in greate measure deprived of a mother's care at a time of life when it is most needed." After their mother's death in 1777, the children came under the supervision of a housekeeper until their father remarried in 1779.

From the age of five onward, Eli, the oldest child, thus

had responsibilities thrust upon him. His concern for his younger brothers and even more for his sister Elizabeth stayed with him into adult life. But far from burdening him unduly, early responsibility hastened his maturing. "He was remarkable," his sister wrote, "for thinking and acting for himself at the age of ten or twelve years." And she observed, "Brother Eli was when young of a mild disposition — possessed a great measure of affability." His parents thought him slow in learning to read, but exceptionally quick at figures. At the age of twelve, furthermore, he commanded "more general knowledge than men considered of the first standing in the country." Elizabeth averred, "In whatever he undertook he seemed to have the sagacity to perceive probable consequences."

In young Eli this intellectual grasp was combined with extraordinary manual dexterity. His father, like many another enterprising New Englander, had his own workshop on the farm to make household furniture and farm gear hard to obtain and expensive to have repaired at the village smithy. Whitney's shop was equipped with a lathe for turning chair posts and with a number of tools for making wheels, and here the boy learned while still very young to fashion a variety of articles. One story tells of his interest in the mechanism of his father's watch, a curiosity that once overcame his veracity. Pleading illness one Sunday morning, he stayed at home while the family was at church, took the watch apart and had it reassembled in working order by the time his father returned. The neighbors marveled at the violin he made when he was twelve. It was "in every part like a common fiddle and made tolerable good musick." Engrossed in making things in the shop, he found little satisfaction in farm work, although, like every New England farm boy, he had certain assigned chores — in winter watering and foddering sixty head of cattle before he set off for school, in summer perhaps helping get in the hay.

Both before and after their mother's death, their father was the center of the children's existence. A heavy man weighing nearly three hundred pounds, he worked his farm, held town office frequently, served for years as a justice of the peace, and throughout his life kept the devotion and respect of his family. While his education was better than that of many of his neighbors, clearly it was his character rather than his attainments that led his children to take counsel with him. Never well-to-do, he represented common sense. They could rely upon his affection. Testimony to the deference his oldest son always accorded him lies in the full letters Eli, Junior, wrote him long after the younger man had made his mark in the world.

When Eli was fourteen, his father remarried. Mindful of the Puritan upbringing that had taught them to respect their elders, the children permitted themselves no criticism of their stepmother. In rural eighteenth-century America, remarriage was the customary solution to a widower's problem; his children would ordinarily fare better. Years afterward, however, his daughter betrayed her feelings: she depicted her stepmother as a cold, ungenerous person. Resentment of the woman who took her mother's place in her father's house no doubt colored Elizabeth's portrayal of her stepmother. Judith Hazeldon Whitney brought with her to her new home two daughters by a previous marriage. Perhaps the contrasts between her eleven-year-old Hannah, "one of the most hairbrained creatures ever known," and the young Whitneys made it difficult for her to accept her stepchildren; perhaps her behavior toward young Eli offended his loyal sister more than it did the boy himself.

His stepmother seemed to have disdained Eli and "his sayings." Vastly proud of a case of knives she owned, she was irritated at the boy's repeated statement that he could "make just such ones if I had tools and I could make tools if I had tools to make them with." When she broke one of the blades and Eli made her an exact duplicate lacking only the stem, she was pleased, and did not thereafter "deride him when he told her what he could make." As for Eli himself, whatever the discomforts to which she subjected him, as a boy and man he avoided allusion to them. After he left home, in writing to his father he always sent his "respects to Mama."

The events of the Revolution directly affected this household. The shot that was heard around the world was fired scarcely thirty miles from Westborough. Volunteers hurrying to join the Continental Army passed through the town. The children heard tales of British raids and the battles fought, of the bitter winter at Valley Forge, the victory at Saratoga, and eventually the capitulation at Yorktown. The entire family in Westborough felt the pinch of hard times, the scarcity of goods and hard money, the drain of war upon every producer. But the Revolution also gave Eli his first business opportunity by making the price of nails high.

However little he may have known of battles and politics, the lad sensed quickly how to put his own talents to use in the emergency about him. His father agreed to his proposal to install a forge in the workshop and let him make nails there. He had his regular chores to do and school to attend in the winter, but he contrived to find time to forge nails, make tools for his own use and perform various services, such as putting in penknife blades for the neighbors. As the work proved remunerative, the fourteen-year-old boy undertook to expand his enterprise. Telling his sister of his plan, but pledging her to secrecy, he set off on horseback to find an assistant. Another hand in the shop, he reasoned, would use no more fuel, and the greater output would increase profits. He was gone three days, and upon his return announced that he had traveled forty miles into the country, in visits to many shops had acquired enough information to pay for his trip, and had hired a helper to come for a month. His father disapproved Eli's three-day absence without permission, but found no fault with the results of the journey. The hired man worked three months for his young employer in Westborough.

Westborough, some thirty miles inland from Boston, lies on the eastern section of the Massachusetts plateau that separates the coastal region from the rich bottomlands of the Connecticut Valley. Worcester County is sandy and infertile. Today it encompasses miles of thinly populated, rather barren farmland interspersed with industrial towns and cities. Not, to be sure, the only home of "Yan-kee ingenuity," this unpromising stretch of country pro-duced gifted mechanics and "tinkerers" almost from its earliest settlement. Thomas Blanchard, inventor of the gunstocking lathe; Aza Waters, who patented improve-ments to the power-driven trip hammer; and Elias Howe, of sewing machine fame, were but a few of a notable group. The shops Eli visited in his search for a helper doubtless contained some clever laborsaving devices, just as the men he talked with were surely skilled in their trade.

But if contriving and making do, inventing and putting the homemade invention to use were not uncommon prac-tices in central Massachusetts, few men had as yet looked beyond the needs of the moment to organize enterprises with potentialities for growth. Pooling of knowledge in the interests of fostering an industry was unthought of. Every artisan kept his special processes to himself, believing "trade secrets" more profitably hoarded than shared, since a rival might offer in exchange less than he got. In extract-ing information from the craftsmen he visited, sixteen-year-old Eli may have given them ideas of his own. More probably they merely thought him too young to regard as a competitor.

It was in his perception of "probable consequences," in his awareness of the necessity of flexibility in meeting changing conditions, that the boy outdid his adult neigh-bors. At the end of the war, when English nails dumped in the American market stripped the profits from local producers, dozens of small New England shops closed down. Young Eli merely shifted his product. Hatpins for women's bonnets, men's walking sticks turned on the lathe — these articles were still in demand. The acumen he displayed at the age of sixteen led him later to undertake musket manufacture when building cotton gins appeared to hold no future for him.

No explanation of what persuaded the young man to seek a liberal education appears in the surviving Whitney papers. He was nineteen, his sister recalled, when she first heard him speak of his wish to attend college. He had had only the schooling the town could offer. He had carried on his work on the farm and run his shop. Peace had come, and the attempted adjustments to the new order were troubling the countryside. Debts burdened New England farmers. In central and western Massachusetts discontent was growing, to break into civil war under Daniel Shays and his associates in 1786. And young Whitney chose the fall of 1783 to ask his father's concurrence in his plan to prepare for college. Perhaps it was his vision of the difficult years ahead for farmers that inspired his determination to leave the farm. Perhaps it was only with the coming of peace that he saw clearly the limitations that life in Westborough would impose. He had no taste for political maneuverings; he showed no sympathy with the violence of protests against the established order which were arising in the hills to the west. Through the shop he had already widened his field of activity. How could he broaden it further at home?

His stepmother from the first opposed his proposal. His father hesitated. A college education was costly, and money in those hard times was not easy to come by. The young man would have to prepare before a college would accept him. Eli himself found the answer to the preliminaries. He answered the advertisement for a schoolmaster in the neighboring town of Grafton, and, to the astonishment of his father, received the appointment. Before the term opened, and as it progressed, he studied diligently to keep ahead of his pupils. His success was such that the selectmen reappointed him for the winter to come. More immediately important, since the town provided his board, the seven dollars a month he earned met his expenses for the summer term at Leicester Academy. During the next three years he alternated between studying at the Academy and teaching school in the towns nearby: in summer a student; in winter a teacher. From qualifying in the eyes of selectmen for teaching reading and writing, he moved forward to teaching arithmetic also, and in 1788 Benjamin Conklin of Leicester pronounced him *"a person of good Sober life & conversation and well qualified to keep a Grammar School — having acquired a good acquaintance with the Latin & Greek Languages, & also with the English Grammar — at Leicester Academy."*

It took effort to progress so rapidly. Although his mind was not exceptionally quick, he brought to bear upon every problem a steady, concentrated attention. Only a man of powerful will and keen intelligence could have met the demands upon him. As a teacher he faced long hours in bare schoolhouses, often icy in bitter weather despite the blazing logs in the fireplace. Pupils were not always docile or parents well disposed. The Bible, the

Psalter, the *New England Primer* and probably Noah Webster's *Spelling Book* were the works from which he taught. No American text in arithmetic existed before 1788. He showed his pupils how to shape a quill into a pen and thereafter required them to cut their own quill pens modeled on the one he had demonstrated. The scene he described briefly when he took leave of teaching suggests the impression his personality had made. At the closing exercises, with parents as audience, "We had a Spelling Match, Red &c &c — After pronouncing a benediction &c &c I bade farewell. It was rather a moving scene — not an Eye in the House but was moisten'd." As a student at the Academy, he worked equally hard, though he found time to cement a friendship with Josiah Stebbins, a fellow student. His first vacation Whitney spent in studying with the Reverend Caleb Alexander at Mendon; and in addition he "was striving to find something which would produce perpetual motion." But his health gave way under the strain of ceaseless work. He succumbed to what his sister cryptically described as the "Hypo." In the summer of 1788, while he was at home for a visit, a severe cold and a distressing leg infection overtook him. For several weeks his family despaired of his recovery.

This serious illness may have influenced his father's decision to forward him the money for college. Certainly the older man was indignant when his wife and stepdaughters neglected the patient in their care. His son had shown his determination and ability. His "Preceptor" at the Academy had testified to his excellence as a scholar, a young man who "ought by all means to go to college." His father never explained what brought him to a favorable decision or when he reached it. Young Eli apparently was uncertain of help till the day of his departure for Connecticut. Then in early March 1789 his father drove him as far as Brookfield, Massachusetts, whence he could take stagecoach for the rest of the journey; and, before turning the sleigh back toward Westborough, his father "payd all expense — left me the dollars and bid me good by." Massachusetts and home now lay behind the young Whitney.

From Westborough to Cambridge is a considerably lesser distance than from Westborough to New Haven. Massachusetts boys bound for college ordinarily turned to Harvard. The founder and head of Leicester Academy, however, was a graduate of Yale; Ebenezer Crafts may well have urged upon his students its advantages over Harvard. New Haven, a flourishing seaport, was more in touch with the world than was Cambridge. Students from every part of the United States went to Yale. Whatever the causes for his choice of Yale, the results for Whitney were momentous. At every stage of his later life, fellow graduates of the college appeared on the scene to lend him aid at critical moments. Harvard men might have helped him during John Adams's administration; few had influence outside Massachusetts once the Jeffersonians were in power.

It was certainly not difference in curriculum that was decisive. Neither college in 1789 laid heavy stress on science, although the encyclopedic knowledge and insatiable intellectual curiosity of President Ezra Stiles gave Yale some distinction in this field. A generation later, Benjamin

Silliman of the class of 1796 and his younger disciples would make Yale a center of scientific work. In the late eighteenth century, however, Yale was still primarily a training school for the pulpit, for the teacher's rostrum, for the bar and thence for posts of public responsibility. To attend college as preparation for an inventor's or manufacturer's career would have seemed a bizarre notion to the men of the time. Whitney himself had no such thought. He aspired rather to learn the ways of the world, to enlarge his horizons, to find for himself some place of honor. In what direction a college education would take him he did not know; he only knew it would carry him beyond the confines of Westborough and Worcester County.

In March 1789 Whitney, now twenty-three years old, dared not present himself at once to the Reverend Ezra Stiles for the examination that must precede matriculation at Yale. The young man had studied a little geometry at Leicester Academy but chose to strengthen his mathematics before going on to New Haven and the crucial test that awaited him there. He consequently sought out the Reverend Elizur Goodrich in Durham, Connecticut, a scholar whose gifts had brought him "the double office of Prof. of Divinity & Prof. of Mathematics" at Yale. Goodrich was a close friend of Ezra Stiles. When the two men had tied in the election for the presidency of Yale, the mathematician had withdrawn in favor of the more eloquent speaker, Stiles. Whitney spent somewhat more than a month in study at Durham, and his work with Goodrich stood him in good stead. Not only the careful drilling in mathematics and the consideration that Stiles accorded any man recommended by his eminent associate, but the warm friendship that developed between Elizur Goodrich, Junior, and Whitney during the stay in Durham were invaluable to the ambitious young man. On April 30, 1789, when he came before President Stiles to undergo the long exacting examination for admission to the freshman class at Yale, Whitney was ready.

The examination, lasting from early morning into the afternoon, covered the candidate's knowledge of Latin and Greek, his ability to translate and parse, his skill in "Latin prose," his understanding of English grammar and arithmetic. Satisfied with performance in these realms, President Stiles had also to assure himself of the young man's moral character. The astute and learned examiner must have noted Whitney's meager interest in literature and the abstractions of philosophy, his unconcern with the social problems about him; but, as Stiles himself was singularly lacking in aesthetic sense, he would be undisturbed by the candidate's unfamiliarity with belles lettres. Whitney's intelligence was beyond question, his maturity obvious, and he had studied with Stiles's admired friend, Caleb Alexander, and with the distinguished Goodrich. Although the college year was half done when Whitney arrived in New Haven, the President realized that to insist that the candidate wait for the opening of the new term in the fall would be a serious setback for a man already older than most entering students. Stiles permitted him to enroll at once.

So began Whitney's years at Yale. They were years rich in intellectual stimulation, in the pleasures of companion-

ship with other able men, and in the interest New Haven
itself offered. Until he said farewell to his father and set
off from Brookfield for Durham, he had never been more
than a day's journey from home. The differences between
the Massachusetts villages he had known and the busy
Connecticut seaport lay in more than the commercial activities on the city's wharves. To New Haven came merchants who had seen China and the Indies, men of wide
experience, personages important in public life. All comers
remarked the friendly warmth of the community, the mel-
low atmosphere that a man like Whitney, not deeply religious but accustomed to the strict Puritanism of rural
Massachusetts, must have found peculiarly agreeable. The
meetinghouse and the Episcopal church, one or the other
of which all good New Haven families supported and attended, redeemed the city from any air of unseemly frivol-
ity. The college with its learned faculty added an element
of sobriety and discipline overshadowing the occasional
improprieties of high-spirited students. Whitney, intent
on making the most of the opportunity his father's generosity was affording him, apparently spared no time for
things that would not advance him. He made friends, but
the library, the classroom and, above all, the museum
with its "philosophical apparatus" engaged his first attention.

The library contained fewer than three thousand books,
many of them presented in 1733 and thus embodying
none of the discoveries of the mid-eighteenth century, few
of the teachings of the Enlightenment. But among the volumes was a copy of Newton's *Principia*, in itself a priceless

tool in the hands of a young man who had once sought to contrive a perpetual motion machine. The equipment in the museum included an air pump, an electrical machine, a quadrant, a theodolite, a whirling table, and "the mechanical powers," that is, devices that illustrated the principle of the lever, the pulley, the toothed wheel, the inclined plane, the wedge and the screw. To these President Stiles added a small telescope, a micrometer and an orrery purchased from England and delivered during Whitney's second year at Yale. The orrery was a device driven by clockworks to portray the movements of the planets about the earth. Perhaps examination of the micrometer, that simple-looking, ingenious, precise measuring instrument, first gave Whitney the idea he would later develop so brilliantly in the machine tools that made possible manu·facture of mechanisms with interchangeable parts. While the museum's miscellaneous curiosities — the Indian helmets, the tapa cloth from Tahiti, the weapons brought from the far Northwest — attracted visitors, students with a scientific bent found excitement in the instruments which procured, Benjamin Silliman later declared, "some reputation for the College, especially in pneumatics, mechanics and electricity."

President Stiles and Josiah Meigs, professor of mathematics and natural philosophy, conducted the lectures. The three tutors who made up the rest of the faculty supervised students' work and drilled them in grammar and composition, history and geography, disputation and such theology as the denominational college required. If some of these subjects stirred little interest in Whitney, he nevertheless kept pace with his fellows. The inscription written into his copy of the *Catalogue of Books in the Library of Yale-College* indicates his academic standing: "The Authority of the College, induced by the esteem and regard which they have for Mr. Eli Whitney, Junior Sophister, present this valuable pamphlet for the trifling consideration of nine pence lawful money." From President Stiles he absorbed sufficient understanding of the principles of law to enable him in the years ahead to plan his course in the fight for his patent rights. He learned to debate and, when occasion demanded, to turn out the oratorical phrasings deemed suitable for a public address. His only published work, the funeral oration commemorating his classmate Robert Grant, who died in his senior year, bears witness to some command of language, even while the sentiments voiced were unoriginal. "When the all-piercing sound of the last trump shall vibrate through the universe," the declamation ended, ". . . then shall we meet, then shall we rejoin our departed classmates — then may we together mount on virtue's wings, and undismayed securely ride through the universal wreck of glowing worlds to seats of never-never-ending joy." Stiles noted in his diary: "The Oration was well delivered."

Meigs's instruction in mathematics doubtless added to what Goodrich had taught the young man, but from Stiles's lectures he could obtain the knowledge he craved even more deeply. The lectures covered virtually the entire realm of eighteenth-century learning: in addition to other fields, "Language or Philology . . . the structure of the Eye & the Nature of Vision . . . Geometry & Conic Sections . . . the Astronomy of Comets . . . different kinds of attraction, Mechanical Powers, Laws of simple and compound motion, Hydrostatics and Hydraulics, Central Forces, Optics, Electricity, Chemistry." Stiles, who read the volumes of the *Encyclopédie* as they appeared, who avidly devoured the latest books on science, and who corresponded on these matters with Franklin, Rittenhouse, Jefferson and other leading American thinkers — Stiles spread his findings before his students. Measured by the knowledge of the greatest men of the period, Stiles's lectures were sound, informing and stimulating. Whitney could scarcely have found in all America a teacher better able to feed him the intellectual fare he sought.

The farmer's son wanted from college other things also. Although he never stated that he hoped for a place in high society, without certain social graces he evidently believed his talents could not take him far. His family, while respected, carried no great name. He must learn to catch literary allusions, to dress with meticulous care, to exhibit courtliness of manner and to be at ease with the rich and well-born. Because his pen would at times have to speak for him, he must cultivate the art of writing, taking pains not only to express himself clearly but also to make the format neat. His language ordinarily was direct. He learned to conduct himself without embarrassment among people who, through wealth or academic position, at that point in his life were his social superiors. He paid close attention to his personal appearance. He possessed the natural advantage of certain good looks — strong features, pleasing in spite of a long beaklike nose, well-set luminous black eyes, delicately carved lips, a firm chin and a tall well-proportioned figure. Ill as he could afford elegant clothes, for his commencement exercises he invested in silk hose, a new coat, waistcoat, cotton shirt and pantaloons.

He attained also considerable popularity with his classmates. The Phi Beta Kappa Society elected him to membership, in those days not a scholarly distinction but a sign of social acceptability, a mark that his associates enjoyed and liked him. He joined the Linonian Society, which, though organized as a book-buying club open to any student, provided diversion from time to time. Whitney presumably found pleasure in attending the "dramatical exhibitions," the disputations, and other entertainments the Society offered. In any case, to make his way in this new world he had to improve his every social opportunity.

His only serious troubles sprang from his need of money. "I have succeeded very well in my studies," he wrote his father, "and meet with no other difficulties but the want of money, which indeed is very great." His father had promised him a thousand dollars, to be paid over in small sums as the cash came to hand. Students, unless they were to incur interest charges, had to pay the college fees promptly, within two weeks of the opening of each of the year's four terms. Charges for a room in Connecticut Hall, for rental of bed and bedding, for board in the Commons, for candles and fuel, for laundry and for a considerable list of other essentials added to tuition and the cost of books to make a total of nearly four hundred dollars a year. The difference between that figure and what his father could give him the young man had to earn. College hours were long. The day began at five-thirty, at five in spring and in summer, and the leisure or "playtime" allowed students was a scant hour following the noonday meal. How Whitney found ways to earn money in the brief time at his disposal is hard to comprehend. He colored "the outlines and divisions in the maps of Guthry's Geography" for students who paid him for his work, but what he earned from that could not have met his needs. His father, like other American farmers, particularly those whose land was not highly productive, was hard put to raise cash, but he remitted the thousand dollars piecemeal and strove as best he could to save his son expense.

"As to your profession," wrote the older man, "my advice is to look forward and count the cost before you plan on bilding and Consider your Surcomstances for I shall not be able to help you much after you are through College."

At the end of his college course, the young man, having settled his bills at Yale with the last remittance from his father, "gave Notes for his debts in the town and reserved the remainder." He needed some money, his sister observed, "to furnish himself for his future employment."

Before he left New Haven for the six-week vacation that preceded his commencement, he discussed his future with President Stiles. Whitney could therefore assure his family when he reached home that a teaching position in New York was awaiting him after graduation. Relief from the prolonged financial anxieties must have made that last holiday pleasant. He could return with a light heart to the ceremonies of commencement in September. The exercises of that September, 1792, marked a special occasion, for President Stiles had completed a negotiation with the sovereign State of Connecticut, whereby, in return for forgiveness of $40,000 in back taxes, the Yale Corporation would add several state officials to its membership. College President and State Governor, representatives of the church and a host of other dignitaries joined in the celebration. From the baccalaureate sermon preached on Sunday to the formal dinner served to one hundred and forty people in the college hall on Wednesday and the orations and prayers that followed in the afternoon, the days were filled with rejoicing, sometimes solemn, sometimes gay, always colorful. Fifty years later Silliman described to Yale alumni the fireworks of the evening preceding commencement when crowds gathered "to view the illumination of the college windows and the dazzling pyrotechnics of mounting rockets and burning wheels, revolving with blazing coruscations, and fiery serpents flying through the air with comet trains, along the front line of the College yard."

For Whitney disappointment dimmed the splendors of commencement. He learned upon his return to New Haven that the teaching post in New York was not available. President Stiles, after breaking that sorry news, told him of another opening. A Major Dupont, a gentleman from South Carolina, wanted a private tutor for his children. The President had recommended Whitney and "thought it a good offer on the whole." Whitney, feeling he had little choice, accepted. He made no bones about his dismay over the change of plan. The climate of South

Carolina, he wrote his brother Josiah, "is unhealthy and perhaps I shall lose my health and perhaps my life." To his father he wrote with greater restraint. If he found his health declining, he would return. "I hope to save fifty Guineas pr. Year besides my expenses, which is more than I can make in New England. . . . Going so great a distance is attended with many inconveniences and many advantages. I shall have the opportunity of seeing the Country, which is a consideration of some consequence. I can tell better when I get there how I shall succeed. Tho I by no means set out upon uncertainties. I have agreed with Mr. P. Miller, a Gentleman from Connecticut, a man of reputation and abilities." The letter did not explain that Phineas Miller was the manager of the estate of the late General Nathanael Greene. Miller was acting for Major Dupont but, evidently observing Whitney's distress of mind, suggested that he make the long journey South in the company of Miller himself and Mrs. Greene and her family. Whitney agreed; he would thus be spared some loneliness.

Whitney's college days thus ended amid personal troubles. He had the degree for which he had struggled against odds for nine years. He was nearly twenty-eight years old. He was vaguely planning to read law. Opportunities for lawyers in the young Republic were numerous; in Connecticut a shrewd observer noted that the best houses belonged to members of the bar. But a man without capital, indeed with debts to meet, must support himself by other means until his legal knowledge could open to him the doors of that honored profession. The position offered Whitney would pay him eighty guineas a year, and perhaps it would allow him a little time from his other duties to study some law on the side. Yet a place in a rich man's household held few attractions for an ambitious man. Mischance, as he then saw it, took Whitney to the South.

The Invention of the
Cotton Gin

DISASTERS overtook Whitney on his way to the South. He was to meet Phineas Miller, Mrs. Greene and the Greene children in New York, whence they would take ship together for Savannah, Georgia. Whitney sailed from New Haven at the end of September on the regular packet for New York, only immediately to become very seasick and to be shipwrecked during the night when the vessel ran on to the rocks below Hell Gate. Uneasy at an expense he could ill afford, he joined several other passengers in hiring a wagon to take them the six miles to the city. Not an hour after his arrival he encountered a friend on the street, shook hands, and then discovered his acquaintance "was broke out full with the small-Pox."

There was nothing to do but take such precautions as medical treatment could provide. Variolation, inoculation with a serum obtained from a person with a light case of smallpox, appeared to be reasonably safe. Consultation with Miller and Mrs. Greene led Whitney to put himself in the hands of a New York doctor who sub-

jected him to variolation so successfully that he had a
very mild case "with only a dozen pock." Roaming about
the city during the two weeks of his "pox," he spent part
of his time with Mrs. Greene and her family. That generous and charming woman made him welcome, pox and
all, and, learning of his anxiety about the cost of his illness and the delay in departure, offered to lend him the
money for his passage to Savannah.

The southward voyage gave Whitney, despite six days
of seasickness, opportunity to become better acquainted
with the woman who had befriended him. Catherine
Greene was only twelve years his senior, but that gap widened by her knowledge of the great world, by the distinguished name she bore as the widow of the beloved Revolutionary war hero, Washington's quartermaster general,
and, most of all, by her sex. Her gallantry of spirit during
the gloomy winter at Valley Forge had fortified her husband and his fellow officers and won her the admiration
of General Washington himself. From Newport, Rhode
Island, where she summered, to Mulberry Grove, the
plantation in Georgia, she commanded the devotion of
countless friends. Widowed in 1786 at the age of thirty-
three, she faced rearing five children and the problems of
a debt-ridden plantation with magnificent courage. If she
used her undeniable fascination to obtain services from
the men about her, her warmth, sweet temper and generosity of heart more than balanced the account.

Although Whitney could not at once have perceived all
the facets of her character, he could feel her charm. She
was a creature new to his experience. His sister Elizabeth,

his stepsisters, and his stepmother had been the only women he had known well. His friends were men. And the gaiety of Catherine Greene, whose example, as she once said, could teach him "how to enjoy the few fleeting years which any can calculate upon," was infectious. Reared in a Puritan atmosphere, Whitney was astonished at the lighthearted aura that enveloped Catherine. She, on the other hand, was quick to see his quality. The diffidence and New England reserve of the attractive young man may have amused her, but her insight enabled her to sense his strength of character, respect his intelligence and to take pleasure in his society.

Arrived in Savannah after seven days aboard ship, Whitney spent but one night in the city before acting upon Mrs. Greene's invitation to visit at Mulberry Grove. In a long letter to Josiah Stebbins, his close friend of Leicester Academy days, he remarked that Savannah, with its ill-built houses and weather-beaten look, had not matched his expectations, and the country roundabout produced crops very different from New England's. At the end of a week at Mulberry Grove he planned to cross the Savannah River into South Carolina and begin his work as tutor to Major Dupont's children.

He did not carry out that plan; he remained as Mrs. Greene's guest at the plantation. At the time he told no one his reasons. Months later he explained to Stebbins that Phineas Miller had misunderstood Major Dupont's offer, and the tutorship would have paid only forty guineas a year. Whitney did not add that he had a more rewarding task in hand. He found no fault with Miller.

On the contrary, the letter declared, "He has really treated me very much like a Gentleman." And Whitney had occasion to know.

Phineas Miller, Connecticut born and educated at Yale, had come to Georgia in 1785 at the request of General Greene to serve as tutor to the Greene children. Upon Nathanael Greene's death the next year, his widow had asked Miller to manage the plantation. Mulberry Grove, presented to the General by the state in grateful acknowledgment of his services to Georgia during the Revolution, had suffered from ten years of neglect. The mulberry trees that had given the plantation its name no longer supported silkworm culture, but with proper drainage and dyking the fields would produce corn and rice. The labor involved was tremendous. Greene, who had made himself individually responsible for the costs of feeding his hungry troops during the last months of the war, had worked himself to death in efforts to restore the plantation. Since Congress had made no move to reimburse him, his estate was burdened with debts.

Phineas Miller thus stepped into a task of utmost difficulty. A loyal friend, gentle, affectionate and high-spirited, he was also hard-working, conscientious, and resolute. In later years, when Whitney gave way to despair, Miller maintained his faith in himself and refused to let Whitney's chidings spoil their relationship. Miller's graciousness and cultivation fitted him for a place in the world Georgia planters would create as cotton brought them wealth. In 1792, society in the deep South was still rather simple — lacking money and rooted in meagerly productive land. At the time of Whitney's arrival, Miller was struggling to make Mulberry Grove pay. But he was no mere overseer; he was a well-loved member of the household.

To Whitney, accustomed to the frugality of his father's household and inured to economies during the lean years in New Haven, life at Mulberry Grove was truly luxurious. Household slaves ministered to the comforts of the family and guests, while the labor of field hands on the plantation's broad acres provided the fare for a generous table. For the debts of the estate did not shrink Catherine Greene's hospitality. The spacious, comfortable plantation house — "magnificent," General Greene had called it — was open to all his friends and to those of his widow. Guests came and went in a never-ending stream. Whitney quickly discovered that, mere acquaintance though he was at first, his prolonged visit at Mulberry Grove was a matter of course to Catherine's neighbors. But for a New Englander to linger on month after month was unthinkable unless he had some reason for staying. From early November 1792 to April 1793 he communicated with neither his father nor his own friends, and when at length he wrote to Westborough and to Stebbins in New Haven, his letters were still mysterious about why he was tarrying in Georgia.

The undertaking that held him at Mulberry Grove during the winter and spring was a closely kept secret between his hostess, his new friend Miller and himself.

There were subtle indications that he welcomed any pretext to justify his spending months in Catherine Greene's
society; but his character would not have permitted him
to enjoy so long an interlude as Catherine's guest pursuing purely personal goals. He justified his presence by
the knowledge that he was serving her interests as well as
his own. A common venture was on foot, a venture she
had inspired almost by chance because she wished to call
attention to Whitney's talents. She had observed the skill
of his fingers as well as the clarity of his mind. He had
made for her a new tambour, a frame for holding needle-
work, and the originality of its design and the perfection
of the workmanship had stirred admiration in everyone
who saw it. Consequently when neighboring planters
calling at Mulberry Grove fell to discussing the difficulties
facing the South and speculated about what a machine
that could clean upland cotton of its seed would mean to
the region, Mrs. Greene remarked to her visitors that
Whitney, who could "do anything," was the person to
whom they should turn.

Whitney had never seen a cotton boll and had scarcely
listened to the talk around him. But when his hostess proposed, albeit without undue urging, that he try to devise
a machine, he pursued her suggestion; he could, he
thought, return to his law studies. Six months later,
a working model of a cotton gin stood in a locked room at
Mulberry Grove.

Whitney's own account of these months, as he wrote the
story in September 1793, omitted many details. He outlined to his father the problem upland cotton posed, its

seed "covered with a kind of green coat resembling velvet," and spoke of the consensus among the planters he had met at Mrs. Greene's that a machine to clean cotton expeditiously would be "a great thing both to the Country and to the inventor." A few days after his arrival at Mulberry Grove he "involuntarily happened to be thinking on the subject and struck out a plan of a machine" which he communicated to Miller. The overseer was pleased and suggested that Whitney experiment further, offering to bear "the whole expense," in return for a share of the profits.

"In about ten days," Whitney's account continued, "I made a little model, for which I was offered, if I would give up all right and title to it, a Hundred Guineas. . . . I concluded to . . . turn my attention to perfecting the Machine. I made one before I came away which required the labour of one man to turn it and with which one man will clean ten times as much cotton as he can in any other way before known and also clean it much better than in the usual mode. This machine may be turned by water or with a horse, with the greatest ease, and one man and a horse will do more than fifty men with the old machines. It makes the labour fifty times less, without throwing any class of People out of business."

This summary, while describing his ultimate success, gave no clue to the steps by which he had arrived at a workable method of ginning short-staple cotton. Despite the plan early "struck out" in his head, months of hard work lay between the idea and the completed model. Phineas Miller turned over to him a room in the basement of the plantation house in which to carry on his experiments, and, shut up there day after day, the subject of much curiosity and some "raillery" from the Greene children, Whitney built his first gin.

When he began his task, he had never seen the "old machines," which, operating on the roller principle, were merely refinements of the *churka* used in India for centuries past. (The word "gin" was apparently a contraction of engine.) The machine used in the South consisted of a pair of wooden rollers grooved lengthwise and turned by a crank much as is a clotheswringer. As the crank revolved the closely set cylinders in opposite directions, long-staple cotton fed into the gin passed between the rollers, but the smooth black seeds caught in the grooves and dropped out. In 1790 Dr. Joseph Eve of the Bahamas and Augusta, Georgia, had made considerable improvements in this gin which permitted it to be run by either horse or water power and, some people claimed, made it possible to clean short-staple as well as Sea Island cotton. No evidence, however, supported that claim; the tight-clinging seeds of upland cotton either broke between the cylinders and scattered fragments through the fibers or passed through with the cotton. The roller principle nevertheless lent itself to a new application. This was Whitney's starting point.

His innovation initially lay in two features of his machine — teeth to tear the cotton from its seeds and a slotted iron guard, its slits wide enough to admit the teeth and the cotton fibers caught on them but too narrow to let the green seeds through. The seeds dropped into a box

below the roller. Ten years later, in explaining why he
used wire instead of anular iron plates for the teeth, he
testified "that I had recourse to wire to make the teeth
from necessity, not being able to procure sheet iron or
sheets of tined plates — that one of the Miss Greenes had
bought a coil of iron wire to make a bird cage and being
embarrassed for want of sheet iron and seeing this wire
hanging in the parlour it struck me that I could make
teeth with that."

The problem remained of how to keep the fibers
caught on the teeth from rolling around on the cylinder
again and again until they clogged the machine. Just as
wire for a bird cage gave the inventor one idea, so a hearth
brush, according to legend, supplied the plan of brushes
to clear the cylinder. None of Whitney's written statements alluded to the source of the idea of using rotating
brushes, but popular stories insisted that he owed it to
Catherine Greene; she had found him puzzling over the
problem of clearing the cylinder and, picking up a brush
from the hearth. playfully asked him why he did not try
that. The idea was almost certainly his own, but whoever
or whatever inspired the scheme, the finished model carried a second, smaller cylinder set with bristles. By means
of a fairly simple arrangement of belts, the crank that
turned the toothed cylinder simultaneously revolved the
smaller brush roller faster and in the opposite direction,
in such a fashion as to sweep the clean cotton from the
teeth. This ingenious adaptation of the roller principle,
obvious enough once seen in operation, constituted the
third essential feature of Whitney's gin. Anyone who saw

it could understand its workings; anyone equipped with simple blacksmith's and carpenter's tools could build a rough copy.

Miller and Mrs. Greene were delighted. Although only they had entered the workshop while Whitney was building his model, now that he had proof of its efficiency, his hostess was eager to show it to "gentlemen from different parts of the South." Stories of what followed vary. Whitney's letters tell nothing of how word of his achievement spread. To display the machine prematurely was dangerous. Yet he may have felt obliged to accede to Mrs. Greene's wishes, and perhaps, too, was anxious for the assurance the endorsement of planters would give.

They gave it wholeheartedly, for when they saw that the gin would "separate more by one hand in a day than formerly in the space of months," they urged the inventor to take advantage of the new Federal law to obtain a patent. If Whitney until that moment had had doubts about the pecuniary value of his work, such advice must have dispelled them. In writing to his father of his plan to undertake the business of building gins, he remarked, "Tis generally said by those who know anything about it, that I shall make a Fortune by it." While thus tacitly admitting that others had learned of his secret, he besought his father to say nothing until the patent was in hand.

At the time of Whitney's departure for the North, only a few friends of Mrs. Greene had viewed the model at Mulberry Grove. Whether or not Catherine Greene saw in this local publicity some element of risk, Phineas Miller, like Whitney, quickly recognized it; the very excitement the planters evinced was a warning. And Miller had a personal stake in the future of the gin. He had already shouldered Whitney's expenses, such as they were, during the winter's experiments, and now that experiment had yielded to proven reality, he had offered Whitney financial backing. On May 27, 1793, four days before Whitney left Mulberry Grove, Miller and Whitney came to an informal agreement. Miller was to meet the preliminary costs, and if Whitney could build machines that worked like the model, "the profits and advantages arising therefrom, as well as all privileges and emoluments to be derived from patenting, making, vending, and working the same, should be mutually and equally shared between them." Whitney was to apply to the Secretary of State for a patent and then begin constructing gins.

Although the most sanguine American in 1793 could not have envisaged the future of American cotton, faith in the usefulness of the gin nursed hopes in the prospective partners. Hamilton's *Report on Manufactures,* widely read during the preceding eighteen months and pondered throughout the United States, might well persuade men of means in America to try cotton manufacture on a considerable scale. Samuel Slater had broken the British monopoly on textile machinery when, after slipping out of England with his specialized knowledge in his head, he successfully duplicated the Arkwright spinning frames and installed them in Moses Brown's factory in Providence. Surely a domestic market for raw cotton would widen rapidly as other Americans followed the Rhode Islander's lead. True, in the "Manufactory at Providence," which Alexander Hamilton had held up as an example, Moses Brown refused to use upland cotton, because, he contended, the dust clinging to the fibers spoiled the cloth. True, also, Southern planters were doubtful about the value of the green-seed crop; in 1792 they had raised over two million pounds only to find that inability to clean much of the pick had left most of it unsold. Even in 1794 John Jay of New York would still be so unaware of the importance of American cotton that he would negotiate a treaty with Great Britain listing cotton among the commodities American ships would not carry to foreign ports. The Senate would reject that crippling clause. Meanwhile Miller and Whitney could believe that they held the key to making green-seed cotton an asset.

Irrespective of markets at home, growing demand abroad promised as ready sale for well-cleaned short-staple cotton as for the long-staple, Sea Island variety. World production of all cotton had stood in 1790 at 490 million pounds, scarcely a million and a half pounds United States grown. In 1792 the United States had exported only 138,000 pounds, all of it long-staple. But it was not want of buyers that had kept the tonnage low. English spinners would purchase as much as the New World could raise, provided the fibers, short or long, were properly cleaned. Miller and Whitney had no exact figures on the size of crops in the South, but common sense could tell them that output of upland cotton waited only on profit, and profit for planters awaited an efficient gin.

While Whitney cautiously observed in the summer of 1793 that some unforeseen contingency might "frustrate my expectations and defeat my Plan," he had reason to add, "I am now so sure of success that ten thousand dollars, if I saw the money counted out to me, would not tempt me to give up my right and relinquish the object."

Ten thousand dollars in the 1790's was a very large sum of money. The figure was a measure of Whitney's belief in his work. At last he saw his future clearly. The plan of becoming a lawyer had vanished. He had prepared for the profession without enthusiasm, thinking only that it might bring him honor, social standing and money. Teaching had been a stopgap while he felt his way toward another career. Now he knew what path he would follow. He could imagine its rewards. He could quickly pay off his debts and, as not only inventor but also producer of the machine that might easily revolutionize agriculture in the South, he could expect a comfortable income, possibly great wealth. His work would increase prosperity at home and perhaps enhance American prestige in Europe.

As he thought of the course before him, he may have wondered why he had not perceived it before. His boyhood training in the workshop on the farm, however limited the scope, had given him practical experience; although machine shops in the United States were still little more than blacksmithies, he had learned the art of handling tools. His studies at Yale had added understanding of scientific principles and theory. His work in Georgia had called upon both types of knowledge. Henceforward he would use all the wisdom he had acquired to forward the novel career that his special talents had opened out to him.

The seven months at Mulberry Grove had done more for Whitney than reveal to him the direction in which he must go. The admiration his gin had elicited had given him the incomparable boon of confidence in his abilities; the approval of men of some importance in Georgia was reassuring to a newcomer. In Catherine Greene's household he had learned much of the great world. At Yale he had known other students, scholars and theologians. The guests who came and went at Mulberry Grove were men of affairs, friends and fellow officers of the beloved Nathanael Greene, men who carried heavy responsibility and filled posts of honor in the new nation, gently bred people of varied background and interests. Phineas Miller was well informed and agreeable, in many ways a model to copy. And there was Catherine herself. Whitney had been shocked at first at some things he observed. A letter to Stebbins dated November 1, 1792, hinted at the New Englander's feelings: "I find myself in a new natural world and as for the moral world I believe it does not exist so far South." Somehow Catherine eventually tempered that harsh judgment. Meanwhile she taught Whitney that, despite anxieties, life offered innocent enjoyments that the Puritan too often ignored. She introduced him to a society where manners were of the first importance and helped him take his place there with dignity. As the years went on, his gifts would doubtless have opened many doors to him unaided, but Catherine

Greene's tutelage while he was still an obscure young man eased his way. Thus tutored, he need not dread approaching the great and famous Jefferson himself.

Whitney said farewell to his friends at Mulberry Grove on June 1, 1793. Scarcity of materials in Georgia and lack of skilled help led him to turn northward; in New Haven he could better obtain what he needed. He sailed from Savannah for New York and thence took stage to Philadelphia, seat of the Federal Government, there to tender his application for a patent and to pay the thirty-dollar fee the law required. His formal letter addressed to Thomas Jefferson, as Secretary of State the official then charged with receiving such petitions, was brief. "Humbly" he stated his wish to obtain "an exclusive property" in his gin. He declared it new in its principles of construction, fifty times as efficient as any machine then used in ginning, and able to turn out cotton containing fewer broken seeds and impurities than that cleaned by other processes. He petitioned therefore for letters patent granting him, "his heirs, Administrators & assigns, for the term of fourteen years the length of time stipulated by the Act the full and exclusive right & liberty of making, constructing, using and vending to others to be used, the sd. Invention or Improvement."

With the application filed on June 20, Whitney could do no more in Philadelphia until he had completed specifications and drawings to support his claim. Before submitting these, he felt he must re-examine every detail of his design, partly to ensure that an enlarged model would develop no weakness undetectable in the original, and partly to work out an expeditious method of duplicating his machine. The enthusiasm of the Georgia planters who had witnessed his model perform made him realize that demand for his gins would be great and insistent. He could not meet that demand by building machines one by one by hand. He must devise some means of producing them in quantity. The difference between a "bench model" and a "production" item is familiar to manufacturers today. In the eighteenth century when *manufactures* still meant to most Americans literally "goods made by hand," only a man of insight could perceive that he must reduce to a set routine every process of fabrication if he was to turn out rapidly replicas of a "laboratory" model. No matter how simple his original design, he must evolve a careful system of reproducing it accurately. And the dearth of skilled workmen in the United States heightened the problem.

Whitney spent a fortnight and more in New York accumulating supplies hard to get in New Haven, and one day drove out to inspect the "cotton works at Turtle Bay," where cotton ginned by his machine was being tried. He purchased files and pliers, a compass and ninety-six pounds of iron wire. As he would need more than ninety-six pounds of wire before he could set the hundreds of teeth into the large cylinder he planned to construct, when he arrived in New Haven he bought materials to build his own wire drawing block. He entered into a small "Expence Book" his every expenditure. He could account to Phineas Miller for every penny, for the cost of his passage and freight charges, for board, lodging and other personal needs, and for the sums paid out for labor and materials to complete the equipping of the New Haven shop. During the summer, in addition to constructing the wire drawing block and plate, he built a lathe and a special turning tool of his own design. Other than hammers and chisels, saws and files, he could buy no tools. He had to make them by hand, just as he had cut and threaded every individual screw. Although severe headaches and illness, possibly a touch of malaria, slowed the progress of his work, by early fall he had satisfied himself of the adequacy of every feature of his gin and was ready to send off the drawings and description to Jefferson in Philadelphia.

In the capital, yellow fever had been raging since August. It drove thousands of people out of the city and, before the epidemic ended in mid-November, caused four thousand deaths. It "so interrupted communication and deranged business of every kind," wrote Whitney to Jefferson on the 15th of October, "that I thought it best not to send my description till the disorder had in some measure subsided. But as the sickness, which I hoped would be of short continuance, still prevails, and as I am unwilling to delay any longer, I herewith enclose and forward it, together with a short description designed to form the schedule annexed to the patent.

"It has been my endeavor to give a precise idea of every part of the machine, and if I have failed in elegance, I hope I have not been deficient in point of accuracy. If I should be entitled to an exclusive privilege, may I ask the favour of you, Sir, to inform me when I may come forward with my model and receive my patent."

While awaiting Jefferson's reply, Whitney took the precaution of preparing a sworn affidavit testifying to the originality of his invention. Elizur Goodrich, Junior, son of his onetime tutor and now an alderman of New Haven, stamped the paper with the notarial seal on October 28, 1793. Whitney's statement included a long description of the gin, its frame, its revolving cylinder studded with sharp wire hooks set at a carefully figured angle, its stationary slatted breastwork, its "clearer" armed with bristles, and its hopper to hold the cotton to be cleaned. This paper, and a second, briefer description, dated the following March and labeled in Whitney's own hand "The True Copy," were his safeguards against mishap to the data he had sent to Philadelphia. Not only was the sworn statement later to prove useful to the inventor in his battle in the courts, but inasmuch as fire destroyed the Patent Office in 1836 and, with it, the official records and model, these declarations, contained in a bound copybook among Whitney's papers, constitute today the only firsthand evidence of what the original gin was like. The short description concluded:

The cotton is put into the Hopper, carried thro' the Breastwork, brushed off from the teeth by the Clearer and flies off from the Clearer with the assistance of the air, by its own centrifugal force. The machine is turned by water, horses, or in any other way as is most convenient.

There are several modes of making the various parts of this machine, which together with their particular shape and forma-

tion, are pointed out and explained in a description with
Drawings.

Jefferson, who had remained in Philadelphia throughout the plague, acknowledged Whitney's letter and drawings in November. The Secretary of State assured the inventor that in order to obtain a patent he need now only
send a model of his machine to be lodged with the Government. The Virginian, however, was more than officially
interested in the gin. He inquired whether it would be
suited to family use, for in Virginia household manufacture of cotton was common, "and one of our great embarrassments is cleaning of the cotton of the seed." Had the
machine been thoroughly tried, he asked, and what quantity of cotton did it clean on an average of several days
when worked by hand? What would a hand gin cost?
Could he purchase one? And was this the machine adver-
tised the year before in Patterson, New Jersey?

Whitney replied promptly that the New Jersey gin was,
as far as he knew, merely the "common" gin improved by
the multiplication of small rollers. His own machine was
not that. He had made his first small, imperfect model
within ten days of turning his attention to the problem
of cleaning cotton, but the gin he had finally completed
in Georgia the preceding April had a cylinder twenty-six
inches long and six inches in diameter. One man operated
it. On the other hand, gins three times as large could be
readily made. Over a two-week period, one Negro had
daily cleaned sixty to eighty pounds of cotton, weighed
after ginning. "The machine cleaned fifteen hundred
weight in about four weeks, which cotton was examined

in N. York, the quality declared good and sold in the market at the highest price. . . . After the workmen are acquainted with the business, I should judge, the *real* expense of one, which will clean a hundred Wt. Pr. Day, would not exceed the price of ten of those in common use." Whitney and his associate had not yet decided at what price they would sell their gins. It would be low enough to make the purchase attractive, but since they would put the first large gins to work at Mulberry Grove, they would be unable to have machines for sale that winter. A gin for household use was certainly feasible; it need occupy little more than two cubic feet of space. By substituting for the clearer three or four cylinders with card teeth, moreover, the machine could card the cotton and deliver it from the gin ready for spinning. Within a few weeks he would bring his model to Philadelphia, and Jefferson could then examine it himself.

Whitney, for all his eagerness to secure his patent and to show his gin to Jefferson, was unable to keep to the schedule he had planned. Construction of the large cylinder proved troublesome. When he drove the hundreds of wires into the wood parallel with the grain, every kind of timber he tried sprang under the strain. At last he arrived at a solution. He built a special machine for cutting the wire teeth; it cut "equally on both sides, feeds itself and goes remarkably easy.' This self-feeding machine tool has not survived, so that whether he copied a device developed by someone else, or adapted to his purpose techniques he had learned in nail making as a boy, remains a matter of speculation. His brief comment reveals only that he was evolving essentially modern industrial methods of production. He discovered that driving the wires thus sharpened across the grain of the wood prevented buckling of the cylinder. These problems solved, in February 1794, he completed a miniature model to deposit in Philadelphia and six large gins to take to Georgia. President Stiles, to whom he demonstrated the machine, remarked it "A curious & very ingenious piece of mechanism."

Whitney took the final steps in getting his patent in March 1794. When he arrived in Philadelphia, Jefferson was out of office and returned to Monticello. The two men would not meet for another seven years, and then on an occasion as significant for Whitney and the nation as that of displaying his newly perfected cotton gin. The new Secretary of State, Edmund Randolph, had a number of leading men in the capital inspect the model before he issued his letters patent. Since the Comptroller of the Treasury, Oliver Wolcott of Connecticut, to whom Whitney carried a letter of introduction from Elizur Goodrich, was greatly interested in promoting invention in America, he may well have witnessed a demonstration of the gin. As a Yale man, class of 1778, he would have had special interest in the work of a fellow alumnus, particularly one so warmly commended by Goodrich, and in the years to come Wolcott's endorsement would more than once be of service to Whitney. On March 14, 1794, Randolph granted the patent. The work of sixteen months thus ended in triumph.

In a letter to his father written from New Haven at the end of March, Whitney indicated the measure of his success:

I have accomplished everything agreeable to my wishes. I had the satisfaction to hear it declared by a number of the first men in America that my machine is the most perfect & most valuable invention that has ever appeared in this country. I have received my Patent. I have also obtained a passport from the Secretary of State to go into foreign Countries & also a particular letter of introduction from Mr. Randolph, Sect. of State, to Mr. Pinkney Minister Plenipotentiary for the U.S. at the Court of London.

Whitney explained that he must go to Georgia to deliver the six large gins he had finished and would then sail direct to England. He concluded:

Though I have as yet expended much more money than the profits of the machine have been heretofore, and am at present a little pressed for money, I am by no means in the least discouraged. And I shall probably gain some honour as well as profit by the Invention. It was said by one of the most Respectable Gentlemen in N. Haven that he would rather be the author of the invention than to be prime minister of England.

Whitney's elation was natural. For himself he had won honor and prospects of wealth. He had vindicated his father's faith in him. For the South he had created a source of prosperity. His gin reduced labor fifty-fold without putting anyone out of work. Indeed, his invention would make employment for thousands — Negro slaves on the land, women and children in the factories, eager white men in the shops and the countinghouses. Trade with England would flourish. The United States would grow rich. In the plantation country men would soon reject as folly the mere thought of emancipating African slaves. The old and feeble, once a grievous burden to their masters, would be put to running gins; young slave boys could help. Whitney could not have envisaged the full sweep of the future. In his first flush of triumph, he thought of himself, his family and friends. Yet his work would have consequences long outlasting his life. His invention would help bring a new society into being and fasten slavery upon the South for three generations to come.

The Career of Miller & Whitney: The Fight for a Legal Monopoly

PHINEAS MILLER had not waited for the formal award of the patent to tell the South of the gin. He had put a notice in the *Gazette of the State of Georgia* on the first of March announcing that he would gin any quantity of green-seed cotton on a basis of one pound of cleaned cotton for every five pounds delivered him in the seed. He added, rashly as events were to prove, that before the next harvest gins to run on those terms would be erected in various parts of the country. Since five pounds of cotton in the seed reduced after cleaning to about one and two thirds pounds, the proposal meant that three fifths of the entire upland crop would go to the planters, two fifths to the owners of the patented gins. While the advertisement did not expressly state that only Miller's establishments would own and operate the new machines, that was the plan he had in mind. He had determined the principles upon which he intended to conduct the business and promised extensive operations before the partnership came into legal being.

Explanations for his precipitate action are clear. In March 1794 he felt impelled to encourage planters to turn to cotton at once: for if they were not to miss a year, they would have to plant in April, and they needed assurance that they faced no repetition of 1792. That year they had suffered heavy losses because of inability to clean and market the green-seed cotton they had raised. Miller had to overcome his neighbors' reluctance to try so risky a crop again. Furthermore, the state of Georgia had offered a prize for a usable gin, and he was calling attention to Whitney's claim to the award. Whitney, if dubious at first about the wisdom of Miller's stipulations, soon concurred in all the arrangements. He accepted a thousand dollars from his friend for a half interest in the patent, and the two men signed the partnership papers in June 1794.

Although Miller had valid reasons for announcing promptly the birth of a new industry, justifications for his particular plan of running the business are difficult. Upon his decision and the partners' long-enduring refusal to revise it hung the fate of their enterprise. No doubt Miller considered the scheme prudent and necessary, and some of its features were. In other respects it was disastrous.

The arrangement to accept payment in kind was obviously sensible. It was a familiar practice in rural eighteenth-century America; flour millers for generations had taken part of the grind as their fee, and sawmills, woodworking shops, fulling mills and other industries often operated on the same principle. No cash changed hands and, since hard money was scarce, the system was direct and simple. By following it, Miller and Whitney shared the risks of their clients and, as it were, pledged their own profits that the output of the gins would be salable. The charge was high, but the partners never admitted that it was exorbitant. They remembered the struggles of perfecting and building the machines and believed that without them Southern planters could not hope for prosperity.

The plan to confine the business to the partners' ginneries also had precedent and, as an opening gambit, logic. Other patentees here and abroad, when able to do so, frequently chose similar methods of exploiting new inventions. Initially necessity dictated Miller & Whitney's decision not to build machines for sale. Miller undoubtedly realized that few planters could buy the gins outright: four or five hundred dollars apiece, the price at which they would have to sell, was prohibitive. In addition, Miller's bold promise notwithstanding, Whitney knew he could supply very few machines for some time to come. He could not train workmen overnight. The shop in New Haven was sparsely equipped, however advanced for its day, and "tooling up for production," Whitney had learned, would take a long time. The factors that militated against selling affected equally the leasing of gins. Unless the shop could turn out machines in quantity neither leasors nor lessees would benefit. Miller's capital, moreover, while seemingly adequate to launch the business, was limited by other commitments, and Whitney had no money at all. Consequently the firm could not afford to wait for accumulating rentals. Both men evidently counted on the profits from ginning to keep the shop running and to provide for expanding operations.

A more significant question is why the partners did not immediately license others to build and sell the patented gins. That arrangement would have solved the problem of supplying machines, furnished the business with some ready cash and kept patrons' good will. Perhaps Whitney's troubles in completing his model led him to think no one else could make it properly, despite its admirable simplicity. Perhaps he and Miller felt that, by licensing, they might lose their just due; and about what constituted justice their idea was fixed. Throughout their lives they would vigorously repudiate the accusation that they were striving to monopolize American cotton processing. Call it monopoly or call it "exclusive privilege," they sought in fact to control an industry. This determination to direct the development of an important new undertaking was the source of their severest troubles.

The stated policies of the firm, however injudicious, nevertheless had the sanction of law. Official letters patent giving an inventor exclusive rights in his creation for a limited number of years were a device the Government used to encourage the "mechanical arts." The purpose of the patent act was "to promote the general welfare" by fostering national industrial growth. Corporate charters of the era not infrequently carried clauses protecting new enterprises from competition until they were well established. A patent similarly was a legalized short-term monopoly, and people, recognizing it as such, usually considered it proper. But unlike most inventions, the gin at once appeared to spell the difference between prosperity and poverty for an entire region. Opposition to Miller &

Whitney's patent arose because Georgians came to feel it was crippling the South. The welfare of society, at which the patent act aimed, should take precedence over private interests, a view that has always underlain fights against monopoly. Reminiscent in the 1790's of royal favors to protégés of the crown, a monopoly injurious to thousands of Americans was abhorrent to men who had acclaimed the Boston Tea Party and fought a long war to be free of subjection to special privilege. Rebellion against the ginning monopoly would grow out of spreading conviction that its effects were intolerable. The failure of Miller and of Whitney to grasp the implications of their plan, and later, when the consequences had become abundantly clear, to modify their scheme while they could do so with grace, would cost them the wealth they had hoped to ensure.

Whitney had set out for Georgia in May, intending to sail thence to England to obtain a British patent and to spread the news that the gin was now ready to resolve the problem of supply to British cotton spinners. At Mulberry Grove the machines he had brought with him went into operation that summer. He wrote his father that they performed satisfactorily. He and Miller had 800,000 pounds of cotton on hand to process, and, when the new crop came in, they would need machines enough "to clean 5 or 6 thousand Wt of clean cotton Pr Day, to satisfy the demand." He designed and built a bagging machine that after trial runs at Mulberry Grove, Miller estimated, would enable three slaves to bag as well as gin six hundred pounds of cotton a day. The enthusiasm of influential visitors to whom Miller showed the gins at work warranted belief that the main problem at the moment was supply of machines — not, as Whitney had half-expected, a matter of persuading planters of the utility of the gin.

Under those circumstances Whitney, though barely recovered from "Georgia Fever," saw fit to return to New Haven to manufacture additional gins. The trip to Europe could wait. In New Haven, in spite of epidemics of scarlet fever and "yellow Jack," which for weeks cut the city off from communication with the rest of the United States and laid low some of Whitney's workmen, he completed his "barn," the new building for his shop, and before the end of the year had it largely equipped.

Miller meanwhile undertook to locate and buy sites in the upcountry where waterpower and ever-widening fields of cotton might make ginneries profitable. He had to engage managers to install and maintain the machines and to oversee operations; he had to find masters willing to rent out the services of slaves to man the work; and, because his plan of business was comprehensive, he had to contract with a firm in the North to furnish burlap for bagging the cotton when ginned. Above all, he had to obtain credit to carry the business until revenue came in.

He drove matters forward vigorously, organizing every detail carefully. Whitney had worked out an economical and safe method of crating, packing the parts of two complete machines in three heavy boxes; Miller therefore ordinarily set up gins in pairs, and since a water wheel or a horse could turn two gins as readily as one, he thus halved the cost of power. Besides the five gins at Mulberry Grove, he soon had ten at work in Augusta, four on Upton's Creek near Washington, two at Golphinton, four at Waynesborough and, by the spring of 1796, two more ready to go into operation elsewhere in Georgia, one in Beaufort, South Carolina, and opportunities to erect other ginneries in the Carolina back country. If Whitney could supply enough machines, Miller, though confronted with serious difficulties, envisaged an enterprise expanding yearly.

Unhappily, the output could not keep pace with demand. Calamity had struck in the spring of 1795. While Whitney, who had gone to New York to renew a loan for the shop, lay ill with a return of malaria, the New Haven shop burned to the ground. "My shop," he wrote his father, "all my tools, materials and work equal to twenty finished cotton machines all gone. . . ."

Indeed three thousand pounds would by no means make good my loss. For more than two years I have spared no pains nor exersion to systimatize and arrange my business in a proper manner — This object I had just accomplished — It was the purchase of many a toilsome Day and sleepless night — But my prospects are all blasted, and my labour lost. I do not, however dispair and hope I shall not sink under my misfortunes — I shall reestablish the business as soon a possible, but it will be a long time before I can repair my loss.

The destruction of his tools and the special machines he had built for quantity production was the chief disaster, but so well had he learned the essential industrial techniques that seven months later he was able to ship twenty-six gins from the rebuilt shop.

Miller, endeavoring to stir sympathy in the South, had published the facts of the catastrophe in Whitney's own words, concluding with the assurance that the business would go on. Miller promised to devote his utmost energies to redeeming the loss. "I think," he wrote with determined cheerfulness, "it will be very extraordinary, if two young men in the prime of life, with some share of ingenuity, with a little knowledge of the world, a great deal of industry, and a considerable amount of property should not be able to sustain such a stroke of misfortune as this, heavy as it is."

But Miller could do little to lighten the financial strain on the firm. He had committed a large share of his own resources to speculation in the Yazoo lands in the West, a colossal gamble that might have netted him huge cash profits from manipulation of the Yazoo companies' stock, if revelation of the fraud the companies represented had not forced the legislature and governor of Georgia to withdraw the lands from sale. A "cyclone of anger and resentment" had swept the state when people learned that company agents had bribed legislators to turn over to the handful of men composing the four companies some thirty-five million to fifty million acres of virgin land at a price of about a cent and a half an acre — land that included, as settlers very much later would discover, the incredibly fertile Mississippi "delta."

The Yazoo scandals had direct bearing on the status of Miller & Whitney. Northerners who might have given the firm financial backing had been caught up in the fever of land speculation, as had Southerners, and when the Yazoo transactions stood revealed for what they were, Miller's connection with them angered men who had suffered or who righteously denounced corruption everywhere. Whitney had had no moral scruples about the gamble, for although he had seen its dangers and before the debacle had warned his partner that speculators, increasingly suspect in conservative circles, could command loans in the North only at exorbitant rates of interest, he had argued his right to share Miller's profits from the Yazoo lands. Miller had pointed out in reasonable vein that since Whitney was in no position to support losses, he could not expect gains from his friend's independent business dealings. The inventor thus escaped personal legal involvement in the ensuing scandals. But Miller's part in the deals was well known, and it so immediately affected Miller & Whitney's credit that without collateral from the Greene estate the partnership could scarcely have avoided bankruptcy. Catherine Greene, however, believed in both men and unhesitatingly put her resources at the partners' disposal. She authorized Miller to use the estate funds. The arrangement assumed entire validity when she and Miller were married in May 1796.

Although Catherine's generosity saved the ginning business from early collapse, the financial pressures on the firm heightened month by month. For Whitney the struggle to keep the shop running on precarious credit was bitter, his inability to settle with creditors humiliating. As time passed he grew desperate. Here was a man who but three years before had seen the world opening out before

him with limitless promise. The leading citizens of the
country, recognizing the importance of his invention, had
prophesied that it would bring him fortune and fame. In
September 1795, Yale College had conferred upon him
the degree of Master of Arts, an honor in those days reserved for attainments of exceptional order. That morning as he marched in the commencement procession
headed by the new President, Timothy Dwight, Whitney
must have savored the moment to the full. In spite of the
fire of the preceding spring, that fall he had reported to
his father that the business was increasing at a pace that
precluded a trip to Westborough and left him no leisure.
The letter rang with confidence. Yet in 1797 despair rode
him. While Georgia and South Carolina were turning
mile after mile of the uplands into cotton fields, while
the crop doubled and tripled and still cotton prices rose,
the man who had made green-seed cotton profitable for
planters found his business near ruin.

By 1797 the firm of Miller & Whitney was indeed in
dangerous straits. Twenty-eight of its gins lay completely
idle. In 1794 the horizon had looked cloudless; plain sail-
ing lay ahead. Successive storms now drove the business
toward total destruction. The burning of the shop, Miller's losses in the land gamble, his subsequent costly lawsuits to collect from men to whom he had sold Yazoo
shares and, even worse, the damage to his reputation and
hence to the firm's, all contributed. But had these been
the sum of their difficulties, Miller and Whitney might
have made headway and held to their course. Cotton
growing was spreading rapidly in the South. The

3,000,000 pounds of 1792 had risen in five years' time to 11,000,000, and the price was moving steadily upward, from 36 cents a pound in 1795 toward 40 cents and more. Every gin in America could have run profitably at peak capacity. Nevertheless, the firm, already weakened by reverses, now faced the threat of complete annihilation.

The chief source of the patentees' troubles lay in the Georgia planters' resentment at the fee for ginning. The charge, they felt, was extortionate, the principle wrong. Why pay to greedy monopolists two fifths of every dollar cotton brought the South? Two men would grow fabulously rich at the expense of the producers of that wealth. Pirating had begun almost at once. In January 1795 Miller had learned from the manager of the Golphinton ginnery that rough copies of Whitney's machine were operating illegally in that neighborhood. For the time being, Miller did nothing. Then others appeared elsewhere, perhaps sometimes without initial realization on the part of the planters who used them that the very act constituted patent infringement.

Formulation of a philosophy to justify the infringements followed after the battle was joined; but most of Georgia, once the pattern was set, found reasons to support the popular position. The gin was not original; Whitney had fobbed off a stolen idea as his own. Basic improvements made the gins that rivals were using quite different from Whitney's; his rights were untouched. And, deadliest thrust of all, word circulated that the patent gin injured the fiber, leaving it unusable in spinning ma-

chines, whereas cotton cleaned in other gins came out
strong and even. As these malicious stories reached England, Miller & Whitney found the firm's market vanishing.
"This stroke of misfortune," wrote Miller in the fall of
1795, "is much heavier than that of the fire. . . . Everyone is afraid of the cotton. Not a purchaser in Savannah
will pay full price for it."

The campaign to undermine the patentees' privilege
gained swift momentum. Miller early acknowledged his
mistake of the summer of 1794 when he had shown the
gins at Mulberry Grove to several friends. With no evil
intent, they had disregarded the instructions to say nothing of the marvelous new invention and had described its
salient features so well that even small boys in Augusta
knew that it "had teeth which worked thro' slats, and a
brush. This was easily understood and easily put into
practise when known, for as the excellence of machinery
consists in its simplicity, the inventor derived his principle
credit in reducing his principles to this simple, plain &
easy application." Miller might have added the significant
fact that this simplicity provided the unscrupulous with
another advantage: they needed only a minimum of capital to build workable, albeit clumsy, machines. Yet that
respectable people would question Whitney's rights and
find excuses to steal his reward was an idea Miller had
thought inconceivable.

The temptation nonetheless proved irresistible. The
burning of the shop and of the machines ready for delivery provided a pretext; what men could not buy they

would make for themselves. Armed with the information that had leaked out from Mulberry Grove, obscure and impecunious blacksmiths and carpenters in the Georgia uplands set themselves to building and selling "improved" gins.

Edward Lyon was the first large-scale offender. Legend sanctified picturesque tales: he was one of a group who broke into the gin room at Mulberry Grove at night and carried off the original model; he disguised himself in woman's clothing, gained access to the gin house and so learned the details of the machine's construction. Miller's version was simpler. As early as the fall of 1793, Lyon, pretending to be an emissary of Miller's Golphinton agent, had attempted to make an opportunity to study the gin. Failing in this and unable to learn in Savannah how the machine was built, he eventually found a man in Augusta who supplied the facts needed, facts obtained from men who had carefully examined the gins at Mulberry Grove. Lyon promptly exploited the information, built and sold gins in some numbers, and declared that his were improved models.

A contestant more formidable in many ways was Hodgen Holmes, a humble mechanic whose skill, nevertheless, enabled him to copy Whitney's gin as soon as Holmes had obtained drawings of the parts from men familiar with the details. He varied the construction of the toothed cylinder, however, because cutting and setting the wires was more difficult than using sheet iron with teeth cut in the edge like a circular saw. Whitney himself had originally intended to employ sheet iron but, when he could not buy it in Georgia, had resorted to wire. He had built one model with toothed iron plates but then concluded that wire was better, since, unlike the rigid saws, it would not force knots and "foul particles" through the breastwork. To Whitney's detractors, Holmes's use of saw plates lent color to the contention that this was a new type of gin. As both he and Lyon could sell their crude machines cheaply, Holmes's "saw gins" and Lyon's models operated in many parts of Georgia and some sections of South Carolina before the end of 1795.

Local artisans, in turn, produced similar machines. Claimants to patents for ginning machines sprang up like weeds. While the able William Longstreet, good friend to Miller & Whitney, completed a new roller-type gin for Sea Island cotton, Dr. Eve, Robert Watkins and others contended over rights to machines supposedly redesigned to clean green-seed cotton. "Improvements" and price wars between producers multiplied confusion. Miller's published warnings that users of illegal gins must desist or face prosecution went unheeded. When the Federal Government granted Holmes a patent in 1796, many Southerners persuaded themselves that Whitney's claims were now only pretensions and his rights nonexistent. Miller & Whitney's "exclusive privilege" was gravely imperiled, perhaps already lost.

Still more alarming to Miller was the possibility that English purchasers would persist in refusing cotton ginned in the patented machines. That falsehood and calumny were at the root of British attitudes was no consolation. The shorter fibers of green-seed cotton required adjustment of spinning machinery set to handle long-staple cotton. Had Whitney followed his first plan and gone to England in the summer of 1794, the firm might have escaped endless trouble. Foreign yarn mills needed cotton, and proof that well-cleaned short-staple cotton, ginned in the Miller & Whitney machines, lent itself to mechanized spinning with minor modifications in processing would almost certainly have prevented the growth of prejudice in England against cotton cleaned by the patented gins. As it was, evidence accumulated during 1795 that the slanderous reports from America were taking effect abroad, deceiving Europe completely. English spinners accepted other machine-ginned cotton, rejecting only Miller & Whitney's. Miller concluded that Whitney must set sail at once. He alone could convince English technicians and capitalists that the patent gin turned out better cotton than could any of the pirated models. British understanding of the truth was vital to the future of the partners.

Whitney saw the wisdom of Miller's arguments, but it was not easy to leave the shop. It could not run itself, and its continued output might be as essential to the survival of the business as ensuring the English market. Heavy debts also stood in the way of his departure. He was incensed at the vicious traducing of his good name and the studied belittling of his work. While he sought to make arrangements for the journey abroad, he assembled testimony from English-trained cotton spinners in New Haven that cotton cleaned in his gin was perfectly satisfactory and, in fact, because they could eliminate one entire operation in thread making, they were willing to pay two cents a pound more for his cotton than for that ginned in the usual way. These statements appeared in full in the *Georgia Gazette* in November 1795. Other New England mills were equally enthusiastic.

Unfortunately, the American industry was small, and its endorsement could not tip the scales in Miller & Whitney's favor. Throughout 1796 Miller repeatedly urged Whitney to sail immediately, and Whitney struggled to find ways to do so without sacrificing more than the firm could stand. He asked Josiah Stebbins at one point to take charge of the shop but quickly withdrew the proposal upon discovering that he could not pay Stebbins's salary. By 1797 neither partner could raise money enough to take Whitney to Europe. Miller had been using every penny he could borrow to buy cotton in order to keep running the gins the planters were boycotting, and even an offer of 30 per cent interest on a thousand dollars to cover Whitney's expenses proved vain. The plan dropped. Whitney never went to England.

Phineas Miller was a sturdy fighter. He knew that Whitney had contributed more than he to their joint enterprise. It rested, he once wrote his friend, on "your genius and my patronage." Although the three to four thousand dollars he had expected to invest had run to more than twelve thousand before the end of 1795, and although, as he explained, his "too ardent" disposition had led to errors of judgment which had cost Whitney dear, Miller was not only resolved to redeem his mistakes but was dedicated to defense of the principle he thought involved.

Like most Americans in that age, he believed in the sacred rights of property. The law had accorded Miller & Whitney a property in the gin. He refused to believe the courts would not uphold that right or that law-abiding citizens might not accept the decision. Since warnings to trespassers had been futile, in early 1797 he prepared to sue Lyon and his associates. Whitney, consumed by his profound depression and residing eight days' journey from Georgia, left the conduct of the case to his partner. Miller professed confidence in the outcome.

In mid-May he wrote Whitney of their defeat. Miller had taken, he thought, every precaution. He had obtained from his agents in Georgia the names of men who were installing or using Lyon's gins. He had engaged in various enterprises to raise the cash needed to prepare the legal evidence of trespass. He had pleaded with English spinners to try Miller & Whitney cotton, so that no obstacle to prosecution of the patent ginning business would remain, once the thieving Lyon and his supporters were confounded. He had twice entertained at dinner the judge who was to hear the case, and the judge, having seen the merits of Miller & Whitney's position, had instructed the jury to observe them. The jury, made up of local men, had nevertheless brought in a contrary verdict, and public sentiment, sustaining the planters' pocketbooks, had found nothing amiss.

The triple damages Miller had expected to collect were now unavailable to bolster the firm's credit. One plantation of the Greene estate, heavily involved in Miller & Whitney's finances, had already gone down at auction for half its worth, and Miller knew now he could not retrieve it. But he would resume the fight. The judge had refused a new trial on the grounds that a flaw in the wording of the Federal patent law made another hearing futile. By error, the revised act of 1793 defined patent infringement thus: "If any person shall make, devise, and use or sell the thing so invented." Substitution of *or* for *and* would have given the plaintiffs a sound basis for action, but as they could only charge the defendants with using the gin, the case fell apart. The judge urged Miller & Whitney to apply to Congress for a rewording of the statute; otherwise, he feared, their cause was lost. The outcome of four years of effort seemingly hung upon an *and*.

Miller continued to bring suits for trespass, but he followed the judge's advice in appealing to United States senators for means of redress. He described the methods by which cotton growers defied the intent of the law. Since legal codes in the Southern states refused to admit the testimony of slaves in court, white men would "procure a machine and immediately put it into the second story of a building, to which they give admittance to no person but their own slaves." As no one whose sworn testimony would be valid saw the gin at work, "it then becomes impossible formally to prove in a Court of Justice facts which may be indubitably known to a whole neighborhood." Years later Whitney wrote Robert Fulton, another harassed inventor:

In one instance I had great difficulty to prove that the machine had been used in Georgia & at the same moment there were three separate sets of this machinery in motion [within]

50 yards of the building in which the court sat & all so near that the rattling was distinctly heard on the steps of the court-house.

When Miller's counsel, remarking the strength of local prejudice in Georgia, advised against instituting new proceedings against an ever-lengthening list of offenders, Miller used that evidence to persuade Congress to amend the law. Revisions voted in April 1800 struck out the injurious clause.

In the three years intervening between the first adverse decision and the enactment of a law that offered the patentees some protection, Whitney's part in the business virtually ceased. What use to build gins that would merely stand idle? If demand developed, those on hand would suffice. As 1797 came to a close, Whitney for the time being washed his hands of the entire miserable affair. Drawing himself out of his Slough of Despond and turning his talents in a new direction, he prepared to open the second and more brilliant chapter of his life. Miller, so far from protesting this shift as defection, must have welcomed the lightening of his anxiety for his friend. Determined to keep the ginning business alive and to nurse it to strength, Miller himself stayed with the fight. To do so, he had to devise new weapons.

He arranged with Catherine's son-in-law, Jonathan Nightingale, to explore Tennessee, Kentucky and western Virginia for possible markets for patent-ginned cotton. The trip brought in nothing, and by November 1797 three hundred "surreptitious" gins of Lyon's make were operating in the Georgia upcountry. Miller nevertheless still felt sure that not all states would follow Georgia's example. Supported by that faith, he turned for help in another direction.

At this dark moment, it was again a Yale man who came to the rescue. Russell Goodrich, a classmate of Miller's, agreed to traverse the West at his own expense in search of the markets Nightingale had failed to find. Goodrich also failed, but both then and later his loyalty was heartening, and his advice was sound. He encouraged Miller in a plan reluctantly devised soon after the loss of the first lawsuit: "to sell the privilege" without selling the gin. Since people in the back country preferred to make their own machines, licensing manufacture promised to be the most profitable method of conducting the business. "The prospect of making anything by ginning on toll in this state," wrote Miller from Georgia, "is at an end."

In early 1799 Miller announced the new policy. When opportunity presented, he would sell gins, but the firm would also sell rights to manufacture and would lease machines. Goodrich had pointed out that renting even for a year would be "a beginning to turn the stream," and Miller had swung so far from his earlier position that he set the price for licenses at a modest figure — as little as two hundred dollars for an entire county. The new terms brought some results. He found buyers for gins, and he obtained at last favorable comments from Liverpool on the quality of cotton ginned in the patented machines.

As indications grew that the stream was indeed turning, Miller may have regretted not shifting course earlier. For, over the years, the strong current of hostility which ran against the patent had done its owners irreparable damage. To meet pressing debts, Miller had put Mulberry Grove up for auction. The great plantation sold in 1800 for a mere fifteen thousand dollars. Yet Miller never lost heart. He and Catherine removed to Dungeness, another plantation of the Greene estate, and he carried on the struggle from there. Backed by an adequate Federal law, he launched a new series of lawsuits against trespassers — against Hodgen Holmes, Edward Lyon and a number of others.

Georgia cried out indignantly at what her cotton growers dubbed Federal coddling of private monopoly: "a manifest injury to the community," proclaimed the Governor, "and in many respects, a cruel extortion on the gin holders." Fortunately for Miller & Whitney, South Carolina saw things differently.

The first purchasers of the gin when Miller offered it for sale had been South Carolinians unwilling to join Georgians in "pilfering" from the patentees. Hodgen Holmes lost his case in South Carolina and was forced to pay for a license. The older state had a long and honorable past. In the autumn of 1801 her leading citizens appeared ready to persuade the legislature to buy rights to the use of Whitney's invention. Jubilant at the turn of fortune in prospect, Miller besought Whitney to come South at once. At the legislative session in Columbia the inventor could best represent the firm, and no opprobrium attached to his name, as it did to Miller's whose connection with the Yazoo scandals was not yet forgotten.

Thus Whitney resumed an active role in the fight now nearly seven years old.

In Columbia Whitney discovered the nature of the combatants Miller had been battling. Twisted facts, evasions, refusal to believe the amply proved truth — maligners had an audience in Carolina as well as in Georgia. From Timothy Dwight of Yale, from Oliver Wolcott, and from President Jefferson, whom by then he had met, Whitney had carried letters of introduction to influential Carolinians. He needed every aid. His training in disputation at Yale served him well. And the value of his invention spoke eloquently for him. Little by little he wiped away ignorance and prejudice. In February 1802, the South Carolina legislature voted to pay Miller & Whitney fifty thousand dollars for the patent rights to the saw gin: twenty thousand immediately, ten thousand in the autumn, and the remainder soon after. A witness of these proceedings, in writing to Oliver Wolcott of the decision, remarked: "It is with pleasure that I make this communication, because it furnishes proof that the States will do Justice to the talents of our Countrymen; and it will take away the Reproach cast upon republics, that they are never the patrons of the arts, nor the rewarders of ingenuity."

Whitney had hoped for a larger reward; he and Miller had asked for one hundred thousand dollars, even that sum far below the worth of the rights. But Miller, whose experience in Georgia had prepared him for less, rejoiced at the offer. While the bill was under final consideration in Columbia, he took Whitney to see their upcountry ginneries, and the decay into which they had fallen during the years of standing idle shocked Whitney into realizing the bargain with South Carolina wise. He agreed to the provisions the state imposed — namely, reimbursement of the fees for licenses collected in the state from individual purchasers, and delivery of two models of the gin within a reasonable time. The deed signed, he set out for New Haven by horse and "sulkey," as he had come, completing the twenty-eight-hundred-mile journey in early May, 1802.

Six months later he was back in the South; for, as Miller had dared to prophesy, the example set by South Carolina led her neighbor to negotiate for a similar purchase, and Whitney went to Raleigh to close a sale to North Carolina. There he learned the incredible news: the legislature of South Carolina had revoked its sale. The pretext was the partners' failure to observe the letter of the contract; they had not returned the five hundred and eighty dollars paid in for licenses, and Whitney had not delivered the models promised. The true reason was not hard to discover. To Georgia, the purchase by South Carolina had come as a blow. If other states recognized Miller & Whitney's title, Georgia would face the uncomfortable alternative of standing alone without honor or, admitting the knavery upheld by her juries, of retracting her denials and forcing her cotton growers to pay. Opinion within the state was divided, but the irreconcilables had wasted no time. By adroit and specious arguments they had assured South Carolinians that the sale was mulcting them of money they need never remit. Failure to record properly in the court minutes the verdict against Hodgen Holmes had given Miller & Whitney's enemies the loophole they sought: Holmes reasserted his claim to invention of the saw gin, and many South Carolinians accepted his plea at face value. Thus nurtured, the opposition had strengthened rapidly and induced the legislature to rescind the sale. The state, moreover, was about to sue to reclaim the twenty thousand dollars already paid over.

Whitney was stunned, at first disbelieving. Again his invention was denied him. He requested Charles Cotesworth Pinckney to remind the state comptroller of the verbal agreement about delivery of the models; they were to come as soon as Whitney could find time to construct them with all the improvements he had worked out in his mind. For that task he had to perfect new tools in his shop, and earlier commitments to the United States Government forbade his dropping everything else to work on the gins. Miller protested equally vigorously the charge of bad faith in delaying repayment of the five hundred and eighty dollars; ill health of the firm's agent was solely responsible. Miller added a full account of Holmes's unwarranted pretensions. Meanwhile "surreptitious" gins were multiplying in South Carolina, and the partners feared lest North Carolina abandon her plans for purchase. Although North Carolina did not withdraw, for Miller & Whitney the question remained: would the contract be honored? It allowed them, over a five-year period, two shillings six pence annually for every saw used in every gin in the state, with only the sheriff's collection fee deducted. If the royalties were paid, they would help meet the expenses of the lawsuits to come. Whitney was thoroughly roused to the dangers ahead, but in South Carolina and Georgia his good name was at stake. In the new conflict preparing he would not leave Miller singlehanded to outmaneuver the foe.

The year 1803 was filled with bitterness for Whitney in his dealings with the South. To Stebbins he declared that cotton was bringing the region five million dollars annually and a fifth of that sum was rightfully his. Carefully he assembled evidence with which to demolish his enemies. He obtained from Stebbins a deposition attesting to personal knowledge of the invention in the summer of 1793. From James Madison, Secretary of State, he got copies of the description and drawings appended to the patent papers filed with the United States Government. His lawyer, Simeon Baldwin of Connecticut, secured other depositions. Judge Nathaniel Pendleton, the first person outside Catherine Greene's family to see the gin at Mulberry Grove, drew up an emphatic statement of the originality of Whitney's machine. And there was Whitney's own affidavit sworn to ten years before.

Grimly in November he retraced his steps to the South. There new sorrow awaited him. Miller was dead. He had succumbed to fever at the age of thirty-nine; the long struggle for the business, the vilification and the outright threats may well have worn down his resistance. Killed by the hostility of Southern cotton growers, Miller & Whitney was now only a name. Anger and grief lent Whitney's words barbs. His Calvinist upbringing had bred in him belief in the depravity of human nature, and he felt

Georgia planters had given him new proof. He must also protect Catherine's interests.

Yet victory was in sight when Miller died. Tennessee was negotiating to purchase rights at the rate of 37 1/2 cents per gin over a four-year period; North Carolina stood by her agreement; and, while Georgia remained recalcitrant and South Carolina was not ready at once to re-establish her contract, signs pointed clearly to her waiting only to find some way of saving face. Not until the legislative session of December 1804 did South Carolina reinstate the sale.

In a last endeavor to intimidate the inventor, upon his arrival in Columbia state officers had arrested him, ostensibly to collect the twenty thousand dollars paid him in 1802. Whitney stoutly defied them. He declared the tribunal before which he was to appear incompetent to settle the dispute. He restated his intention to meet every condition of the contract but concluded "that to have industriously, laboriously, and exclusively devoted many years of the prime of his life to the invention and the improvement of a machine, from which the citizens of South Carolina have already realized immense profits — which is worth to them millions, and from which their prosperity, to the latest generation, must continue to derive the most important benefits, and in return to be treated as a felon, a swindler, and a villain, has stung him to the very soul. And when he considers that this cruel persecution is inflicted by the very persons who are enjoying these great benefits, and expressly for the purpose of preventing his ever deriving the least advantage from his own labors, the acuteness

of his feelings is altogether inexpressible." The state legis
lature appointed a committee to hear the charges. At a
stormy meeting, attended at Whitney's request by his arch
opponents, he cut the ground out from under their feet.
The committee reported in his favor, and after a few
meaningless phrases of self-justification, the state restored
the grant and arranged to remit promptly the rest of the
money due him. This payment enabled him to turn over
five thousand dollars to Miller's executor to be used on a
"Judgment against the Estate of Genl. Greene." Whitney
asserted, however, that he had spent forty thousand dollars in getting thirty thousand dollars out of the South.

Georgia held out for another two years. Whitney, having remarked the "solemn truth that many Citizens of
Georgia are amassing fortunes, living voluptuously and
rolling in splendor by the surreptitious use of the gin,"
pressed the suits instituted by Miller against dozens of
different trespassers, while the Circuit Court countenanced
various devices to delay a final decision. In Georgia alone
the suits brought by Miller & Whitney between 1798 and
1806 numbered over sixty — a costly and maddeningly futile repetition. But with the money from South Carolina
in hand, Whitney now had financial resources, and, more
important, the weight of public opinion elsewhere in the
South was mounting daily against the one state that refused to do him justice.

The first favorable verdict came in 1806. In May, the
court issued a perpetual injunction against one defendant,
and in December Judge William Johnson gave a decision
against another. Whitney had displayed two models of his

gin, one made with wire teeth, one with teeth cut around the circumference of an iron plate. The judge declared Hodgen Holmes's gin merely an adaptation of Whitney's. "Every characteristic of Mr. Whitney's machine is preserved." And what honest man could deny the value of his invention? "The cotton plant," declaimed the judge, "has furnished clothing to mankind before the age of Herodotus. The green seed is a species much more productive than the black, and by nature adapted to a much greater variety of climates; but by reason of strong adherence of the fiber to the seed, without the aid of some more powerful machine for separating it than any formerly known among us, the cultivation of it could never have been made an object. The machine of which Mr. Whitney claims the invention, so facilitates the preparation of this species for use, that the cultivation of it has suddenly become an object of infinitely greater national importance, than that of the other species ever can be. Is it then to be imagined that if that machine had been before discovered, the use of it could have been lost, or could have been confined to any tract of country left unexplored by commercial enterprise?"

The "very pointed decision," as Whitney described it, gratifying though it was, did not immediately enable him to collect damages in Georgia. Other court actions intervened, but at last a jury awarded him two thousand dollars and costs of the suit, an amount dubbed "triple the damage sustained by the plaintiff."

So ended the long, heartbreaking struggle. Whitney had re-established title to his invention and cleared his name, together with Miller's. For Miller, whose courage had fortified Whitney's and thus made the final victory possible, the posthumous vindication created a place in history. For that small, belated honor perhaps Catherine Miller was grateful. Otherwise the cotton gin brought her little but sorrow. The patent had expired in November 1807, and Whitney's two petitions to Congress to extend it came to nothing. Cotton growers, contending they had already paid handsomely, stood solidly against the proposal. Georgia's delaying tactics, to be sure, had saved her planters from making more than token payment. North Carolina's fees amounted to about fourteen thousand dollars, Tennessee's to an undetermined figure. In addition, the firm took in some ninety-five hundred dollars from sales to individuals, and from the ginning operations at Mulberry Grove. The fifty thousand dollars from South Carolina represented the one substantial sum Miller & Whitney received. All told, the intake reached perhaps ninety thousand dollars, against which stood the costs of manufacturing, shipping and installing the gins, interest on the investment, travel, lawsuits, and the time and energy of the partners.

Then and a hundred years later, Southerners occasionally declared that the Yankee inventor had obtained princely sums from the South, that Northerners' accusations of Southern greed arose from failure to recall the value of money at the opening of the nineteenth century. That argument was two-edged, for the costs of proving Miller & Whitney's right to any payment, judged by the same standard, were very high. Even in the 1790's, no one could bring more than sixty unsuccessful lawsuits without paying out large fees. When the final settlement of the partnership took place in 1818, the referees allowed Whitney eleven thousand dollars solely for the expenses of his six journeys South to represent the firm's interests.

Just as sectional pride rose to the defense of Southern cotton growers' behavior, so sectional feeling from time to time down into the twentieth century would go a step further to resurrect the charge that not Whitney, but Eve, or Longstreet, or Watkins, or Holmes, or any one of a number of men generally long since forgotten, was the true inventor of the gin.

Only one ancient argument dropped out of sight: that the gin was of no importance. Judge Johnson had summarized truthfully the significant facts. Before the invention of the machine, people were emigrating from the South for want of work. "The whole interior of the Southern states was languishing." As soon as the gin appeared, new vistas opened; the entire South changed. Old people and young at once found lucrative employment. "Individuals who were depressed with poverty, and sunk with idleness, have suddenly risen to wealth and respectability. Our debts have been paid off, our capitals increased; and our lands are treble in value." No words, the judge declared, could express "the weight of obligation" which the country owed this invention, and since cotton was rapidly supplanting wool, flax, silk and furs in manufactures, that indebtedness would grow still heavier in the future; cotton one day might even replace specie in the East Indian trade. The Northern states also had benefited. Ginned cotton provided raw materials for their factories and profitable cargoes for their ships.

By 1808 David Ramsay, historian of South Carolina, could repeat without fear of contradiction the statement that land suited to cotton had tripled in value. Eleven years later, at the time of the Missouri Compromise, the United States was raising 180,000,000 pounds of cotton a year, nearly a third the world's supply, and at Whitney's death in 1825 exports of American cotton to Britain alone had reached 171,000,000 pounds. The wilderness of upland South Carolina and Georgia had given way to mile after mile of cotton fields punctuated at intervals by handsome new plantation houses, gardens and outbuildings. Wealth created by virgin soil, black men's labor and a New Englander's invention was strengthening the power of the slavocracy within the nation. Cotton had indeed become king.

What had his invention brought Whitney? Certainly frustration and disillusionment. His bitterness even reached out to Miller fifteen years after that loyal friend's death, for at the final settlement of the partnership, Whitney demanded damages and received seventy-five hundred dollars for injuries he claimed to have sustained from Miller's land speculation twenty-odd years before.

A by-product of the gin and the furies it loosed was the inventor's enduring resentment of the treatment accorded creative talent in America. His belief in the good faith of the Federal lawmakers was badly shaken, if not wholly destroyed, by the readiness with which Congress listened to the specious arguments of men who, in their own interest, opposed his plea to extend the life of his patent beyond the scant fourteen years the statute allowed. In considering public attitudes toward inventors, he shared the anger of Robert Fulton, whose *Clermont* was known from one end of the country to the other and copied as widely, and of the versatile but ill-rewarded Oliver Evans who had provided the machinery to revolutionize flour milling and whose improvements to engines made the river steamboat economically feasible. "An invention," Whitney declared, "can be so valuable as to be worthless to the inventor."

In 1811, when the gin was public property, Whitney wrote Fulton:

I have always believed that I should have had no difficulty in causing my rights to be respected if it [the gin] had been less valuable & used only by a small portion of the community. But the use of this Machine being immensely profitable to almost every individual in the Country all were interested in trespassing & each justified & kept the other in countenance. Demagogues made themselves popular by misrepresentations & unfounded clamors, both against the Right & the Law made for its protection.

Like other inventors of the young Republic, Whitney paid a high price in emotion for whatever he gained.

His analysis of the basic cause of the opposition to his patent was sound: the gin's incalculable value to an entire region. What he failed to perceive was that the needs of society might override individual rights. His statement to Fulton proclaimed Whitney's conviction that greed and self-seeking had motivated planters and politicians who lacked the courage, ingenuity and perseverance to solve their own problems honestly. He himself had known hardship. As a penniless young man he had worked doggedly to perfect his machine. The destruction of his first shop by fire and the loss of credit following upon Miller's gamble were disasters he could not have forestalled. He had endured hunger and loneliness while endeavoring to re-establish himself, only then to find his honor questioned, his contribution to the nation denied. These experiences blinded him to any view but his own: he had earned the rewards accruing from his invention, his property in law, and justice demanded respect for his rights. The South, on the other hand, also had a great deal at stake. There men looked upon the gin as the key to economic survival. A hundred and fifty years later, had the doctor who developed poliomyelitis serum insisted that children receive only injections prepared in a laboratory from which he drew the profits, public indignation would have run strong. Similarly in Whitney's day, although most men believed property the foundation upon which civilization rested, if private interest ran counter to public, conflict ensued. And restriction on the use of the gin threatened the well-being of all the cotton-growing states.

Without the gin, to be sure, those states might have found another road to prosperity, as a century and more later they did. Manufacturing, commerce and a diversified agriculture, though slower to develop, would have built an economy not dependent upon Negro slave labor. But few people of Whitney's generation, once they saw what wealth cotton could bring, put faith in anything else. Whitney suffered from the demands of a society intent upon a single goal.

Yet the cotton gin also won him fame, lost to sight though it was during much of the nineteenth century. The final reckoning would probably show that he netted several thousand dollars, but at the ultimate cost of recurrent illness and death at the height of his powers. The one significant gain proved to be the experience he acquired in the course of establishing his rights. He learned what he must do to put himself out of reach of the envious. He learned where to enlist support for his experiments and money to finance their completion. The equipment in his shop, the industrial techniques he developed in producing the gin, and the organization necessary to maintain a form of enterprise new to the world derived from his apprenticeship in Miller & Whitney. That apprenticeship taught him the lessons essential to success as an industrial pioneer.

V

The First Contract
for Muskets

WHITNEY embarked upon his second great venture at a time when the gin promised neither honor nor
profit, and when his debts were so heavy that he dreaded
an encounter with his friends on the street. While his partner was considering how to salvage the firm, the inventor took stock of his own situation. He could not go on
without money, and the shaky condition of the firm now
stripped him of credit. A man whose failure was whis-
pered about could not borrow from a bank; pride and a
sense of propriety forbade appeals to his friends. And an
emotional crisis in his personal life heightened the wall he
built between others and himself.

Catherine Greene's marriage to Miller in May 1796 had
manifestly come as a shock to Whitney. During the next
year and a half his letters to Miller and to Josiah Stebbins,
now married and moved to faraway Maine, were filled
with partly told griefs. Business worries alone were not
enough to explain them. Doubtless he had never permitted himself to examine closely his feelings toward

Catherine. If reason told him that this woman who spread a web of enchantment about her was his devoted friend, nothing more, emotion nevertheless betrayed him. The gloom that engulfed him smacked of sheer jealousy. In the fall of 1797 he expressed it to Miller, contrasting their lives. One partner was happy in the companionship of a delightful and sympathetic woman and had "estates, separate from this"; the other, who had "ever looked forward with pleasure to a connection with an amiable and virtuous companion of the other sex," could not at that point *"even think* of Matrimony." He added:

My most unremitted attention has been directed to our business. I have sacrified to it other objects from which, before this time, I certainly might have realized 20, or 30, Thousand Dollars. . . . It is better not to live than to live as I have for three years past. Toil, anxiety and Disappointment have broken me down. My situation makes me perfectly miserable.

At that bitter hour everything Whitney had worked for appeared lost. His college education, earned by immense effort and self-sacrifice, had neither established him in a profession nor even provided a livelihood. The talents he had cultivated at Yale and exercised in perfecting the gin and the tools to produce it had had little play in the lean years of financial troubles. Having clung to belief that his invention would win him the place in the world at which his ambition aimed, he found himself at the age of thirty-two drifting, with no port in view. Yet he knew he had gifts he could somehow employ to his own and to others' advantage. His strength of will reasserted itself in late 1797. After casting about in several directions, he at last perceived where his future should lie: he would find his way by using the knowledge he had painfully acquired in the three preceding years.

Analyzing the elements that had brought the ginning business to disaster, he could see that greed and "human depravity" were not solely responsible. Lack of adequate financing had played a part, contributing to the partners' inability to meet demand and thus leaving them helpless against legitimate complaints. He obviously concluded that backing for a new and experimental enterprise could best come from the Government. Merchants' capital accumulated in bold voyages to far parts of the earth was not yet to be risked freely in the uncertainties of manufacturing, least of all manufacturing by an unheard-of method. No matter how approached, the few banking houses and insurance companies were equally unready to invest in what might well be pure folly. With no money of his own and an unsuccessful business past, Whitney knew he could not organize a joint stock company to finance a scheme incomprehensible to most people at the time. Reputable land companies, like the Ohio Associates, could enlist shareholders for settlement of country in the new West, but land was itself an ample security — even if unseen, a tangible, familiar, undeniable asset. He could offer no security. A public institution, on the other hand, would not be seeking profits; for a public purpose it might advance money to a man whose sole collateral was his own proven ingenuity. Thus the United States Government became Whitney's chief hope.

Arrived at that conclusion, Whitney spent the winter of

1797-1798 in taking the steps preliminary to a specific proposal. He designed and built a screw press with dies to be used "for executing the Stamp Act" and in March 1798 sent the drawings and instructions of how to use and maintain the machine to the Supervisor of the Treasury for the district of Connecticut, John Chester. Whitney was too late. Regretfully Chester wrote that the Government had made other arrangements; but he was sufficiently impressed to forward the drawings to Oliver Wolcott, now President Adams's Secretary of the Treasury, and Wolcott, in adding to the official refusal a brief comment about his own high opinion of the inventor's ability, slightly softened the blow. The screw press has long since disappeared. Perhaps Whitney found some other use for it; possibly he disposed of it as an idle exercise of creative talent. But Wolcott's gratuitous notation was encouraging, and the Federal Government had other wants to be filled. On May 1, Whitney in a letter to Wolcott set forth a new proposal. The United States needed muskets; Whitney stood ready to make ten to fifteen thousand.

For early in 1798 war with France looked ominously near. France had once supported the cause of American independence, sent ships and men, and supplied a good share of the shoulder arms for the Continental Army. But France was now under the control of new men and in its own interests was disregarding the rights of her recent ally. In March President Adams informed Congress that the mission of Charles Cotesworth Pinckney to Paris to iron out Franco-American differences had failed. France had gone so far as to announce that her captains would

hang American seamen as pirates if found on British vessels. Excitement and anger mounted throughout the
United States. Must the nation, however ill armed, endure
the multiplying affronts? Anti-Jacobins considered war
preferable.

But American indignation did not equip an American
army or navy, and France was still a great power. When
Franco-American relations had begun to deteriorate rapidly in 1794, the United States had purchased some seven
thousand muskets abroad. In the present emergency, however, she could not hope to procure arms from Europe,
since virtually every nation was preparing for war and
French privateers made safe delivery doubtful. Nor could
the two Federal arsenals, Springfield Armory, founded in
1794, and Harpers Ferry, now but two years old, fabricate
the many thousand stands of arms needed. A stand of arms
meant the musket itself, the bayonet, the ramrod, the
wiper and the screw driver. Skilled Government armorers
had turned out scarcely a thousand in three years of operation at Springfield Armory, and Harpers Ferry was not
yet producing at all. The Government had to call upon
private contractors. These circumstances ensured Whitney's offer a hearing.

Time was all-important, and labor to make the most of
it was woefully scarce in the United States of the 1790's.
Whitney's proposal took both facts into account. To Wolcott he made clear his conviction that he could rapidly produce muskets in quantity by using machines to do much
of the work. An arms contract would enable him to
maintain the work force he had trained, and men taught

to shape metal and wood by machinery would be equally efficient whether their output went into gins or muskets. In describing to Wolcott his plan for musket manufacture, he wrote:

> I am persuaded that Machinery moved by water adapted to this Business would greatly diminish the labor and facilitate the Manufacture of this Article. Machines for forging, rolling. floating, boreing, Grinding, Polishing etc may all be made use of to advantage.
>
> Cartridge or Cartouch Boxes is an article which I can manufacture. I have a machine for boreing wood of my own Invention which is admirably adapted to this purpose. The making of swords, hangers, Pistols etc I could perform.

He would procure, he explained, a good fall of water in the vicinity where he could have works erected in a short time. It would, however, not be worth his while to go to that expense unless he could contract to make a considerable number of stands of arms. He could arrange sufficient bonds for the fulfillment of a contract of this kind and offered to go to Philadelphia immediately to make his proposals.

To Whitney manifestly his plan seemed sheer common sense. He was not thinking at the moment of revolutionizing American industrial methods, though that in fact would be the ultimate result. His first interest was in reestablishing himself and laying the foundations for his own business future. Adaptation of the techniques he had worked out for another purpose was the easiest path. The demand for gins had put pressure upon him to find some way to produce them quickly and in numbers. His letters written after the shop burned in 1795 reveal that even that early he had devised special tools to expedite the work. That location in New Haven had lacked water power. In a shop supplied with power from a water wheel and equipped with lathes, the "machine for boreing wood" and other machines of his own invention, musket manufacture could proceed with the speed the emergency required. His first overture did not specify exactly how he expected to carry out his plan, and whether, when he arrived in Philadelphia, he explained in person the essential features of his scheme is uncertain. All that mattered to him at the time was to convince Federal officials that he could execute any contract they awarded him.

Yet he knew that the method he intended to use was novel, untried in America for anything so precise as the lock of a musket. At no time did he lay claim to "inventing" the "interchangeable system." He would never again attempt to patent anything. His idea, though original with him and born of his experience, was one on which others were working simultaneously. Jefferson later described a workshop in France he had visited in the 1780's, "in which the owner had defined the various parts of his Muskets, on the principles of Mr. Whitney, . . . that his were gaged and made by Machinery . . . that by Authority of this Country at great price he [Jefferson] attempted to remove this Artist to the United States — but he was immediately taken into the service of the Crown, and had since deceased." A French workshop in which precision work was "gaged and made by machinery" was the first place where a man had successfully experimented with what was to become the basis of modern mass production.

Adam Smith's *Inquiry Into the Nature and Causes of the Wealth of Nations,* published in 1776, had extolled the virtues of the division of labor. Translating that concept into mechanized operations was a step logic would suggest to his students and one that British cotton manufacturers were already taking. In shops in Rhode Island machines were performing the more difficult task of automatically cutting and shaping nails and card teeth, but these, unlike firearms, demanded no exact dimensions. A mechanism like the lock of a musket or the works of a clock called for an exactness in the fit of its parts which men still assumed must defy machine manufacture. In the late eighteenth century, precision work, while not precise by the ten-thousandth-inch standards of a later age, was an art, not a craft. The most skilled workman was obliged to file and fit every individual piece in endeavoring to mate the parts of a mechanism. Out of Whitney's belief that he could turn this art into a routine grew his daring proposal to manufacture ten thousand muskets.

Whitney's letter reached Wolcott at a critical time. Congress had just appropriated eight hundred thousand dollars for the procurement of arms, but neither the Cabinet nor the Congress knew where to spend the money. Whitney's offer must have eased many anxieties. If one man volunteered to make 10,000 to 15,000 stands of arms, surely contracts could be placed for the remaining 35,000 to 40,000 the Administration deemed necessary. Wolcott spoke to the Secretary of War of Whitney's "skill in me·

chanick" and urged the inventor to come to Philadelphia at once. Driven by his desperate hope for a contract, Whitney lost no time. The swiftness with which the negotiations then went forward bears testimony to the sense of urgency which pervaded the capital; the Government was as eager as Whitney to complete the transaction. Three weeks and a day after his arrival in Philadelphia, he and Wolcott, as representative of the Government, signed the contract.

Whitney himself drafted most of the terms after consulting by letter with Simeon Baldwin, his New Haven lawyer. Fear of losing this heaven-sent opportunity kept Whitney's price modest, 134,000 dollars for 10,000 complete stands, $4.40 apiece more than the cost of the muskets imported in 1795. Fear of the imminent outbreak of war, a fear heightened by the French privateers hovering off the coast and reportedly even stopping American vessels in Chesapeake Bay, kept Government officials from viewing overcritically a contract they might otherwise have rejected. For, incredible reassurance, Whitney promised delivery within twenty-eight months: four thousand stand before September 30, 1799; the other six thousand before September 30, 1800. The Federal Purveyor of Supplies questioned the time schedule and put into writing his doubts about Whitney's ability to meet it. Who, on the other hand, could do half so well? The contractor was to use as his model and to copy as exactly as possible the Charleville musket of 1763, the type with which France had supplied the United States during the Revolution. United States inspectors, paid from Government funds, were to prove the barrels in lots of five hundred and one thousand, and inspect and prove the finished weapons at Government expense. The United States, moreover, would furnish the stocks, well-seasoned black walnut, at twenty-five cents apiece. Whitney was to receive a five-thousand-dollar advance immediately, and another five thousand as soon as he had given evidence of having spent the first sum in "preparatory arrangements." Upon delivery of a thousand muskets accepted by the inspectors he would get a third advance of five thousand dollars and thereafter be paid for each thousand stands as he completed them.

Although the advances of money were Whitney's first source of satisfaction, the realization that he was now in a position to try out his special scheme of fabrication must have been scarcely less gratifying. It was an exciting prospect, but it also spelled loneliness. In England gifted mechanics were pursuing much the course he set for himself — men of the caliber of John Wilkinson, maker of the first accurate metal-cutting borer, of Joseph Bramah, the locksmith, of Samuel Bentham and Marc Brunel, brilliant designers of machinery for making pulley blocks for ships of the British Navy; and, above all, of James Maudslay, whose slide rest first made available to men seeking to shape iron a machine controlled by gears and a lead screw to turn out rapidly screws and metal parts of extraordinary uniformity. Whitney had no such associates to talk with.

Yet other Americans were interested in similar problems, and scores of men were inventing laborsaving devices, some of them patented, more of them not, some of lasting importance, others primitive and makeshift. But communication was too poor, even between towns in the same general region, to permit one man to learn much of what his neighbor was doing. No better illustration of the isolation of like-minded men from one another exists than the failure of Whitney in New Haven to realize that Simeon North in Middletown, only twenty miles distant, was struggling to achieve identical goals. In the first decade of the nineteenth century, North would begin manufacturing side arms by employing machines and a division of labor to make pistols, component by component, with final assembly then accomplished with little or no filing and fitting. Tradition, indeed, attributes to North's gifted son Selah the invention of the filing jig, matching concave molds to hold the work in fashion that forced the workman to follow the contours of the jig in filing the piece to be shaped. But although North was operating his shop in 1798, he was obscure and unknown to his New Haven neighbor.

The Rhode Islanders who were using automatic machines for nail and card-teeth manufacture were concerned with very simple applications of a system Whitney was intent on elaborating and perfecting. These men and others like them were craftsmen turned mechanics by chance in their search for efficient production of particular wares. Whitney approached the problem more nearly as an abstraction. To him what he made mattered less than how he made it, and he became a manufacturer in the process of putting his special knowledge to work. He established his contacts with famous contemporary mechanics only later in life. His brief correspondence with Robert Fulton and Oliver Evans began in 1808 and 1811 respectively and then touched merely upon the rights of inventors and their hopes of persuading Congress to write a new patent law. After 1815, Whitney would exchange technical information with the superintendents of the national armories, particularly with the able Roswell Lee at Springfield, but by then the inventor would have solved his problems for himself.

In 1798 he was undertaking an audacious new venture. Without benefit of counsel from experienced mechanics, he had himself to devise the instruments to carry it out. His imagination had enabled him to see that machines — equipment a later generation would call "machine tools" — could produce muskets of greater precision than could the most carefully trained hands, and make them faster than could an army of gunsmiths. His ingenuity would enable him to design and construct the machines which, supplementing those he had already built, would perform this miracle of production. Without intellectual grasp he would never have perceived the feasibility of what came to be known as "the interchangeable system"; without courage and self-confidence he would never have tried it; without manual dexterity he could not have succeeded.

Whatever his talents, however great his self-confidence, the marvel nevertheless remains that he dared commit himself as he did in that first contract with the United States Government. It was unlikely that he had ever carefully examined a Charleville musket until he left Philadelphia carrying with him the model he had pledged himself to reproduce exactly. When he signed the contract, he had not yet bought the land on which to build the arms factory; he had still to obtain materials, plan and erect the building, recruit additional workmen and, most difficult of all, design and construct any new machines the work might necessitate. And he had undertaken to do all this and complete ten thousand muskets in little more than two years' time. He must have believed the feat possible; dishonesty was not in him. While admitting the risk to himself, he may have chanced cutting the time short, lest the Government, unwilling to wait, negotiate a large number of small contracts for a few hundred muskets each. On that basis Whitney knew he could not profitably try his new scheme.

Twenty-six other men accepted contracts that year. Between them they were to make 30,200 stands of arms; they would use conventional methods, each workman forming and fitting components together by hand, one musket at a time. In the agreements with these small contractors, the Government used standard printed forms. The fact denoted a routine procedure, though the article to be made was one few Americans had thought of attempting before. The paper Whitney and Wolcott signed, on the other hand, was formally prepared, fully written out, and perfectly explicit. The transaction was neither casual nor hasty, despite the speed of its consummation. The Secretary of the Treasury and the Secretary of War recognized the boldness of Whitney's commitment; they also knew they were dealing with a person of honor. Whitney would fulfill the engagement if anyone could. He did not hoodwink them.

For the United States Government the contract was a gamble well worth the risk.

The weeks in Philadelphia had been strenuous for Whitney. Long hours of discussion, demanding persuasiveness, repeated explanation, and unfailing courtesy, added to the fatigue bred by the tensions of the capital. Ahead lay a unique and difficult task. But as he traveled back to New Haven by stagecoach, he still felt blessed a relief.

Bankruptcy & ruin [he wrote his friend Stebbins] were constantly staring me in the face & disappointment trip'd me up every step I attempted to take. . . . Loaded with a Debt of 3 or 4000 Dollars, without resources and without any business that would ever furnish me a support, I knew not which way to turn. An opportunity offered to contract for Manufacturing Muskets for the U. States. I embraced it. . . . By this contract I obtained some thousands of Dollars in advance which has saved me from ruin.

By comparison with the past, the future looked easy.

If at any time during the negotiations in Philadelphia doubts assailed him about the time he had allowed himself, his actions and his letters in the months immediately following betrayed no uncertainty. But he wanted no interference. When, shortly after his return to New Haven, he learned of a proposal to establish a second arms factory nearby, he opposed the plan vigorously. Contending that it would create unwholesome competition for both raw materials and labor, he explained to Wolcott: "I have not only the *Arms* but a large proportion of the *Armourers* to make." He planned to employ men with families and "perhaps some little property to fix them to the place," but, once trained at his expense, they could strip him of his every profit by demanding sixpence a day increase in wages. A would-be local rival might well try to have musket parts made elsewhere and only assembled in New Haven, where he could lure Whitney's trained workmen away. The inventor of the cotton gin, who had seen imitators exploit his ideas, was unwilling again to expose himself to theft. Answering the argument of the unknown advocate of a single center for the manufacture of arms, he declared:

Birmingham or Sheffield in England would be the best place to establish the business in that country — These observations are just when applied to European countries where particular manufactures have in a course of ages naturally centered in particular places, but in this country and in executing a contract of this kind, which must at all events be fulfilled within a given time, the effect will be directly the reverse. It would be like an attempt to plant a forest with full grown trees.

His objections quashed the plan.

That threat disposed of, Whitney forwarded to Wolcott the bond the Government required as guarantee of performance of the contract. Confidently, the new arms maker planned his next moves. With the advance of five thousand dollars in hand, he undertook to recruit workmen in Massachusetts, while he attempted to complete the purchase of the millsite near East Rock in the town of Hamden just north of New Haven. At the same time, he arranged to send a ship to Philadelphia to pick up four thousand gunstocks from the public stores there before winter closed the Delaware to navigation. Procuring the bond and enlisting a few additional workmen went

smoothly. In every other particular, his carefully laid
plans went awry. Within four months of signing the contract, he had run into obstacles that, he admitted to Wolcott, would delay the work incalculably.

Not until mid-September did he acquire title to the
millsite. It was worth waiting for, but the late date lost
him precious weeks of good weather. The location on the
Mill River which New Haven settlers had chosen for their
first gristmill was the one place in the vicinity ideally
suited to his purpose. Although he found after tearing
down the old corn mill that the ground was so uneven
that he had to lay expensive new foundations, the natural
setting lent itself to efficient use of the power, and the
volume and thirty-five-foot fall of the water ensured him a
steady flow during most of the year. Below the dam, furthermore, the stream was navigable for heavy barges,
while the new turnpike north to Hartford ran near the
river and made land transport easy. The high ridges flank-
ing the valley cut off the biting winds of winter, and the
farm adjacent to the river provided space for living quarters as well as shop buildings.

Whitney had intended to use the ginning shop in New
Haven for part of the work, but a journey to Springfield
dissuaded him. A conversation with the Superintendent of
the Armory and an inspection of the layout there — where
the "water shops" for forging were some two miles from
the finishing shops on the "hill" — convinced him of the
economy of concentrating all operations in one place.
But, despite his best efforts and the number of men he
employed to hurry on construction, the New England win-

ter did not wait. An early snowstorm prevented laying the foundations of the main shop promptly, and it was late January before the building was completed. The premature onset of bitter weather also interfered with the otherwise simple job of rebuilding the dam and the flumes. Soberly Whitney confided to Stebbins, "I have now taken a serious task upon myself & I fear a greater one than is in the power of any man to perform in the given time — but it is too late to go back."

Meanwhile other troubles had arisen. Yellow fever in Philadelphia in the summer of 1798 had driven the Government to Trenton and halted delivery of the gunstocks from the capital. The quarantine also meant that Whitney could not buy iron and steel in Philadelphia. New England ironmasters, he feared, could not supply him materials of the quality he needed. Refined iron from Salisbury, Connecticut, was suitable, but only one man in that part of the country was in a position to furnish barrels ready for boring and finishing, and he could not supply iron for the locks. Most New England streams dried up in summer and left forges to stand idle until late autumn. Quite apart from quality, where was sufficient iron to come from? The length and severity of that winter of 1798-1799, with its twelve heavy snowstorms, affected every producer in the region. Whitney at length wrote the sorry facts to Wolcott.

In the month of February I contracted with Messrs. Forbes & Adam of Canaan, who are unquestionably among the most able and punctual dealers in and manufacturers of Iron in this Country, to make me a number of tools, Mill-iron and other heavy iron work, for all of which I carried them patterns at the time, and to supply me with roll'd iron Rods, etc of a particular description. All these they were to send me in a fortnight. At the time I was there their Works were frozen up & had been somewhat injured by a late flood. . . . I had a letter from them a few days since saying that "their works were much more injured than they imagined" . . . At the same time I contracted with another man in the same neighborhood — a man of property and reputed to be one of the most punctual, to supply me with several tons of iron — all to be delivered in the month of April. The season proved such that neither ore could be dug nor coal burned until all the fodder for cattle was expended, then neither ore nor wood could be transported for the want of teamwork & I have not received a single pound of iron from that quarter. The man with whom I contracted to weld my Barrels failed — this would have been a great disappointment if I had met with no other. . . .

At the time I entered into the Contract to manufacture the arms, my mind was occupied in devising the best & most expeditious mode of doing the work & I contemplated the Dispatch and facility with which I could work after all my apparatus was compleat and in motion and did not sufficiently consider the time that must necessarily be taken up on constructing and making this apparatus. . . . I find that my personal attention is more constantly and essentially necessary to every branch of the work than I apprehended.

Nor was this the full list of his difficulties. In purchasing materials, he discovered that his problems of financing were still unsolved. With Government backing, he had counted on getting commercial loans, only to find that the sixty-day notes satisfactory for merchants were too short-term for a business like his. In commercial transactions, he observed, quick turnover made that credit scheme useful. "But manufacturing is very different." He had to take money earmarked for other purchases to pay off the notes and was unable to buy in the quantity economy dictated. Raw materials had to come from considerable distances, and suppliers needed ample warning of when to make delivery. Urgently he besought Wolcott in June 1799: "Cannot some arrangement be made by which I may obtain such indulgences as will enable me to pursue the business with equal advantage to the Government and relieve me from the extreme anxiety which now in some measure overpowers my ardor and damps my resolution?"

These depressing handicaps notwithstanding, Whitney still professed faith in his methods. While appealing to Wolcott for an extension of time and another immediate large advance of money, he lamented that no opportunity had occurred to show the Secretary of the Treasury the "whole plan & manner of executing the different branches of the work," so that Wolcott could himself compare it with the practices of foreign and other American makers.

My general plan of arrangement [affirmed the contractor] is good my confidence in it increases in proportion as the execution advances. I have about sixty good men engaged and a prospect of being able to procure such number as I may want. I am persuaded that I can do the work well. . . . I might have made 500 stands of Arms by this time but they would have cost me 15 Dollars apiece and would not have been as good as I wish to make them. My Aparatus would have been such that it could not readily have been enlarged with advantage and it would have taken me six months more to make another 500.

He declared himself ready to subject his system to "a strict examination by men of sense & information & stand or fall by their decision."

The modern world understands the meaning of tooling-up for production of arms. Officials at the end of the eighteenth century could not readily comprehend. How could they tell whether Whitney's statements were a combination of puling excuse and braggadocio or were simple truth? War with France still threatened the nation, and the supply of muskets was still alarmingly short. Wolcott, fortunately, was intelligent and, for all his conservatism, farsighted. He recognized the need of domestic manufacture of munitions even as he saw the country's immediate want of arms. "Besides obtaining an immediate supply of arms," he had written in January 1799, "it is the wish of the Government to diffuse such a degree of skill in the manufacture of Musquets as will exempt this country from the necessity of arranging further importations."

In handling Whitney's disturbing request, Wolcott doubtless leaned somewhat upon the opinions expressed by the officer recently appointed to prove barrels and inspect muskets made for the United States. Captain Decius Wadsworth was a good judge of competence and his views carried weight. He was a Yale man, a classmate of Phineas Miller, and had examined Whitney's cotton gin in every detail. His respect for the inventor was heightened by inspection of the arms factory at Mill Rock in the spring of 1799. True, Wadsworth was apprehensive lest the unique method of manufacture he had seen and heard explained after all prove to be impractical, but he had pronounced the muskets Whitney was making in this novel fashion superior to any fabricated "for common use" anywhere in the world. Wolcott knew the Government armories could not meet the country's needs. He believed some contractors would fail to fulfill their obligations. If only by elimination, Whitney became the one manufacturer upon whom to depend.

On July 6, 1799, less than three months before Whitney was to have delivered his first four thousand stands, Wolcott granted the reprieve. Though he declared his skepticism about untried theories and pointed out that the old way of making muskets was effectual, he concluded:

If you feel entire confidence in your project and will furnish me with additional security for a further advance, money shall be granted to enable you to make a fair trial. I should consider a *real improvement* in machinery for manufacturing arms as a great acquisition to the United States. For present purposes & to give you time to look out for good security, I enclose you a [letter] of credit on the Collector of New Haven for 1500 Dlls.

Whitney's letter acknowledging the singular grace accorded him, this extraordinary evidence of trust, mingled gratitude with gratification, while inner certitude impelled him to explain the basis of his faith. In the first draft of his reply, a paragraph later deleted alluded to Wolcott's distrust of theory.

I am fully sensible [declared the innovator] that Actual Experiment is the only true touchstone of theories, the only infallible criterion by which we can discriminate between theories formed on principle and the chimerical projects of a vague imagination.

So far as I have brought my projects to this test I have had the satisfaction to find them fully answer my expectations.

There in two sentences spoke the intellectual and the man with firsthand experience.

By existing practical standards, Whitney had failed. He had not lived up to the terms of his contract; he had not delivered a single finished musket. Although he had an agglomeration of parts stacked in his shop awaiting completion of other components, few men saw in that si - uation any promise for the future. Yet this first large-scale American experiment in mass-production methods ultimately held enormous significance for the country. Out of Whitney's "system" developed the manufacturing techniques that formed the basis of the nation's industrial growth.

V I

The Birth of the "Uniformity System"

WHITNEY's system of manufacture was the result of careful analysis. It required breaking into its constituent parts the article he wished to produce and then devising a series of machines to turn out each component accurately. Other Americans were using power-driven machinery to fabricate relatively simple wares; Whitney successfully applied machinery to the making of intricate mechanisms. In writing to Wolcott in the summer of 1799 the inventor described for the first time the essentials of his plan.

Instead of relying upon "one great complicated machine, wherein one small part being out of order or not answering to the purpose expected, the whole must stop & be rendered useless," he developed separate processes for each individual component. Cutting, grinding or boring, he suited the machine to the piece it must fashion. If experiment showed one process faulty, he could adopt another without changing the method of making other parts. Thus he saved time, money and frustration. The proce dure enabled him to forge the guards of the musket-lock quickly, "and so they will require less work in fitting up than they could be cast in brass after a perfect Pattern by an experienced founder." Similarly the method was advantageous in making several of the smaller "limbs" of the lock and mounting and permitted forging of the "lockplates with a solid pan." The plate, Whitney declared, "I have ever considered the most difficult part of the lock."

Though expediting the work in its early stages was important, Whitney underscored the still greater value of another hoped-for result. "One of my primary objects," he wrote, "is to form the tools so the tools themselves shall fashion the work and give to every part its just proportion — which when once accomplished will give expedition, uniformity and exactness to the whole." As long as each workman depended upon the accuracy of his own hands and eyes to make a component correctly, every piece would vary somewhat from every other. Many parts would need "an inscription upon them to point out the use for which they were designed, & it would require treble the number of hands to do the same work." Every filing operation and hand tailoring to make pieces fit took time, patience and skill. "Long practise," Whitney admitted, might teach a mechanic "the art of giving a particular uniformity of shape to particular substances." But in America men with experience of that kind were few. If the United States hoped to obtain in the near future any considerable number of good muskets made on this side of the ocean, manufacturers would have to resort to new means of producing them. The man-power shortage left no other alternative. Whitney's system, by depending upon tools instead of men, would ensure a degree of uniformity unattainable in weapons fabricated by hand. "In short, the tools which I contemplate are similar to an engraving on copper plate from which may be taken a great number of impressions exactly alike."

While that telling analogy explained the principles upon which he was working, nothing in his long letter to Wolcott gave a clear picture of progress on the contract. On the contrary, in July 1799 Whitney's statements on that subject were confusing. For in discussing the date at which he would make a first delivery of arms, he appeared to deny that his system was in full working order. The phrase, "the tools which I contemplate," was itself disconcerting. Were they still but ideas? Two years and more had passed since he had signed the contract. The noncommittal tone he adopted was even more disquieting to responsible officials.

I shall be able to finish some muskets by the time stipulated in my contract for the first delivery but what number I shall be able to Deliver at that time, I do not undertake to say — not so great a number by any means, however, as I expected — though I shall have some of the smaller limbs of the whole ten thousand made by that time — And I am warranted by experience as to many parts in saying that I can do them as well & with much greater expedition than they have ever been done in this (& I believe) in any other Country — I must also candidly acknowledge that more time must necessarily be taken up in the first establishment of the business than I at first had any conception of — I find it vain to think of employing a great number of hands in erecting the works and making the tools — unless I could actually be present in many places at the same time — I must not only tell the workmen but must show them how every part is to be Done — They are as good as any workmen but I cannot make them understand how I would have a thing done till it is Done.

Wolcott's discomfiture at this vagueness may be imagined, but his terse response merely imposed conditions upon Whitney in return for the extension of time and credit. The contractor must furnish bond to cover the ten-thousand-dollar advance, and he must complete a number of stand before the end of the year when the Secretary of the Treasury would have to report to Congress.

Ten of New Haven's leading citizens — most of them Yale men — underwrote the bond for ten thousand dollars. Although a mortgage upon the shop and farm at Mill Rock offered them security, their endorsement was a mark of their confidence and pride in Whitney. Besides Elizur Goodrich, whose father had tutored the ambitious young man ten years before, and Simeon Baldwin, the distinguished lawyer and Whitney's counsel, the men who stood behind the adventurous manufacturer included James Hillhouse, today chiefly remembered for his planting of New Haven's elms, and Pierpont Edwards, aristocratic son of the great preacher and philosopher, Jonathan Edwards. Whitney could take vast pleasure in the very names of his supporters. Ten thousand dollars released him from immediate financial pressure and left him free to attend to his shop in an effort to finish the muskets Wolcott insisted upon receiving that year.

A sentence in a letter that Whitney saw fit to revise before sending to a Government official indicates that in the summer of 1799 he had not yet equipped his shop with some of the machine tools he intended to develop. He thought better of saying: "I might bribe workmen from Springfield to come & make me such tools as they have there but that would neither correspond with my feelings nor answer my purpose." What were the tools in use in the Government armory which he chose not to copy? The Springfield Armory records that survived a destructive fire of 1801 do not list the equipment at that early date. Nor do Whitney's papers describe the machines he installed at the Mill Rock manufactory. Had he taken out patents on the most important machine tools he designed and built, public records would supply a rough chronology of his inventions, each machine in turn presumably more complex than its predecessors. Probably one of the first innovations he employed was a simple filing jig, a pair of matching concave clamps or molds, the contours of which forced the filer to follow them and thus to shape the work right. From the filing jig to a fixture for holding the cutting tool would be a logical step, though one more easily envisaged than contrived. Obviously, most of the machines were power-driven as early as 1799.

Even then the plant very likely contained a number of machines entirely new to America. A ten-year-old nephew, Philos, eldest son of Elizabeth Whitney Blake, left the one authentic clue to what comprised his uncle's factory in 1801. To his sister, Philos wrote: "There is a drilling machine and a boureing machine to bour berels and a screw machine and too great large buildings, one nother shop to stocking guns in, a blacksmith shop and a trip

hammer shop. . . ." Doubtless the principles of operation of each of these modern-sounding tools were identical
with those of the more exact and more powerful machine tools of today. Blacksmiths in other parts of America may have had crude trip hammers; ironmakers in the
Salisbury, Connecticut, region used them extensively
after 1800. And the possibility cannot be discounted that
the skillful Rhode Island mechanics who produced card
teeth by automatic processes had drills and other power-
driven machines as novel and as admirably suited to special work as were those Whitney designed for musket
manufacture.

Whitney's unique contribution to American industrial
development, however, does not rest upon the characteristics of particular items he devised. It was his execution of
a carefully-thought-out system, of which every separate
type of machine was a part, that ranks him high among
American industrial pioneers.

Like other men after him, Whitney, remembering the
gin, was unwilling to patent his inventions. He preferred
to test his ideas and put his interchangeable system of
manufacture to use for himself. He made no secret of his
innovations. Many people besides Government inspectors went through his shops, and to each of the curious in
turn he explained the equipment and concepts behind it.
He had no fear that others could reproduce these com-
plexities. Indeed, fifty years later, men claiming inventions in the field of firearms would be unable to manufacture accurate first models, so that the United States
Government, hoping to encourage the development of new

weapons, would offer to have Government armorers make the models for test. Thus in 1858 John Brown would submit a "new" pistol that, amid the excoriations "God's Angry Man" directed at Springfield artisans, the Springfield Armory would attempt to construct. Whitney knew that without drawings and specifications the most observant visitor to the factory at Mill Rock could not build the entire series of machine tools which constituted the value of the whole.

The ingenious manufacturer, however, was unable to deliver the first five hundred muskets until September 1801. And ten months before, in November 1800, his bulwark in the administration had resigned in protest at President Adams's policies. Wolcott, unbeknownst to Adams, had been one of the cabal in the Cabinet undermining the position of the President until, in the May preceding, Adams had dismissed all but his Secretary of the Treasury. Wolcott, an impassioned adherent of Hamilton, had consistently stood as a buffer between Whitney and his critics. With Wolcott gone, Whitney could envisage the painstaking structure he had evolved over the years past demolished quickly. He himself had sedulously avoided any political commitment. Yet who but Wolcott in a position of power would countenance further postponement of deliveries, however valid the reason?

In December 1800 Whitney set out for Washington, the new capital on the Potomac to which the Government had recently moved. There he must again establish the soundness of his methods and explain the inescapable difficulties that had piled delay upon delay to leave him without a single stand of arms completed and accepted two months after the day upon which he had contracted to turn over the last of ten thousand finished muskets. Only the fact that few more than a thousand of the thirty-two thousand muskets promised by the twenty-six other contractors were in the Government's hands appeared to plead Whitney's cause.

For the ordeal before him he made such preparations as he could. A letter from Decius Wadsworth would be reassuring to anyone not swayed by prejudice. Of Whitney's work Wadsworth wrote in laudatory terms and, to forestall destructive comment on the seeming unreliability of the manufacturer, declared his judgment, prudence, diligence and intelligence of a rare order. From the Government inspector of small arms in Philadelphia, Whitney obtained a certificate testifying to the excellence of his workmanship, the best specimens "in the fabrication of War Muskets which I have seen." Whitney counted still more heavily upon the evidence he carried with him from his shop, a musket of his own manufacture and samples of locks. These would be tangible proof that he had not wasted his time and Government money. More than words they should demonstrate his accomplishments.

The election of 1800 was past. John Adams, hurt and angry, would be soon leaving the half-finished Executive Mansion, and Republicans, hated "Jacobins" to the defeated Federalists, would be taking over in Washington. The impending shift might increase Whitney's problems. Were he to convince men still in office, might their successors not vindictively repudiate their decisions? Fortunately for Whitney, he found men of both parties ready to listen. Wolcott was still in the capital, a circumstance comforting to his friend, and Elizur Goodrich was in Congress, representing his district of Connecticut. President Adams and the heads of departments gave the anxious contractor a courteous hearing, while Jefferson, the President-elect, displayed an appreciative interest rooted in his all-embracing intellectual curiosity and his knowledge of arms manufacture in France.

That first week of January, 1801, marked the turning point in Whitney's career. No full account gives the details of the drama he enacted. He may have staged his demonstration at the newly finished Capitol, or perhaps in the War Department office at the Treasury, or possibly at the President's mansion. One may picture officials, clad in the blue coats, knee breeches and silk hose thought proper for Federal dignitaries, gathered about a table upon which Whitney had spread out the parts of locks and the musket he had brought from New Haven. As he had foreseen, those samples of his work were the main props of his success. Before the fascinated eyes of his nearly incredulous witnesses, he assembled complete locks by taking parts at random from the pile on the table. Every man present could disassemble and reassemble the locks, substituting components from one to fit into any other of the smoothly working mechanisms. Doing, as well as seeing, carried conviction.

Elizur Goodrich's letter to Simeon Baldwin, written on

January 8, 1801, described the result. Of Whitney's arms he wrote:

They have met universal approbation & are considered as evidence that this Country need not depend on a disgraceful recourse to foreign Markets for this primary means of defence. All Judges & Inspectors unite in a declaration that they are superior to any which the artists of this Country, or importation have brought into the Arsenals of the United States — and all Men of all parties agree that his talents are of immense importance, and must be exclusively secured by and devoted to the means of defence. The arrangements will be made perfectly satisfactory [to] him — and he is requested as the Artist of his Country to suggest from time to time all alterations, improvements &c which may in his opinion, be useful in the Armories of the United States &c.

Jefferson attended the formal gathering of officials to see Whitney's performance, but Goodrich seized the opportunity to take his friend to call upon the famous Virginian. Jefferson, whose wide experience gave his commendations special force, "did not hesitate to say," Goodrich reported, "that he had in no instance seen any work or specimens equal to Mr. Whitney's, excepting in one factory in France. . . ." Jefferson offered to write to Governor James Monroe of Virginia recommending that he engage the New Englander to make muskets to arm the Virginia militia, but Whitney declined to accept further work until he had more nearly completed the contract with the Federal Government. Thus began a relationship founded on warm mutual respect, a personal link between the younger man and the most influential person in America, a statesman whose insights would later save Whitney from many embarrassments.

The triumph of the demonstration could scarcely have been more complete. The "Artist of his Country" was to name his own terms. He requested an immediate ten-thousand-dollar advance, five thousand dollars more three months later and a payment of five thousand dollars upon delivery of each five hundred muskets. He asked for six months in which to finish and deliver the first five hundred stands and proposed June 1803 as the date for delivery of the remaining ninety-five hundred. Acting upon the request that he suggest improvements in design, he added:

The modern French Locks have a brass pan, which has the advantage of not being corroded by the nitre of the powder, of being placed with greater facility in a more favorable position to receive the Fire from the hammer, & of more effectually securing the priming from the rain — which advantages I think will more than compensate for the expence of the alteration. . . . I cannot introduce the Brass Pan at all in the first 1500. But if it should be tho't advisable, I will contract to make Brass Pans to the second parcel of 1500 stands, for six cents each in addition to the contract price, and Brass Pans with an alteration in the hammer, etc so as to embrace all the advantages, to the remaining seven thousand stands for an additional to the Contract price of ten cents on each musket.

The Government accepted these changes in the original agreement. Instead of ten thousand dollars Whitney would have thirty thousand in advance, five years instead of slightly over two. The army would get better weapons patterned on improved models more easily maintained in the field. The United States was not yet at war, and prospects looked somewhat brighter for avoiding open conflict altogether. The nation, in short, could afford to wait for muskets so clearly superior to any others purchasable at home or abroad.

The one flaw in the fabric woven by a wise Government and a conscientious contractor was the knot created by the extreme caution of the new Secretary of the Treasury. Upon Wolcott's resignation, President Adams had appointed Samuel Dexter to the post. Dexter, who for some months had been Adams's Secretary of War, felt he knew how best to protect the interests of the army. Whitney had elaborated for him the principles of the interchangeable system and the problems attendant upon introducing it. Whitney's letter avowed the maker's initial ignorance of arms manufacture but explained that he had benefited from employing workmen who were not trained gunsmiths, so that he had been able to instruct them in his own methods. He personally had had to supervise the making of every pattern and mold. "My system I now consider as established and my theory successfully reduced to practice." Dexter was not wholly convinced. He delayed sending Whitney the promised ten thousand dollars until the end of February and raised objections to forwarding the five thousand due in April.

Jefferson intervened. Inaugurated in March, he replaced Dexter at the Treasury by appointing Albert Gallatin, but, because Gallatin disapproved of large military expenditures, transferred supervision of the contracts for small arms to the new Secretary of War, Henry Dearborn. Dearborn had had wide military experience and knew the army's needs — not penny-pinching, but good weapons.

When he examined the contract records and found that Whitney had received thirty thousand dollars of Government money and had delivered no muskets at all, the Secretary wrote to inquire the meaning of this extraordinary situation. Whitney repeated for him, as for Dexter, the tale of trouble and frustrations but also restated the ideal and the degree to which the shop in Connecticut was approaching its realization. More heartening, he announced that he would have five hundred muskets ready for delivery in July, that some components of several thousand more were nearly finished, and "some of the limbs of each of the whole ten thousand are now made." Dearborn was satisfied. On September 26, the first five hundred arms were fully proved and inspected, at the proving house Whitney had erected by Government request and at Government expense at Mill Rock.

A long road still lay ahead, strewn with obstacles and hazards, but Whitney's future was no longer in doubt. Dearborn found his muskets good. The factory, if not fully equipped, was in smooth running order. The "system" was a workable reality. Government armorers and private manufacturers were beginning to seek the innovator's advice. His word was sufficient to introduce modifications to standard arms. He had won approval for a method of packing the muskets which would protect them from rust. His concern to get well-seasoned pine boxes carefully fitted and designed to keep dampness from the weapons anticipated by more than a century the preoccupation with packaging which would engage the attention of munitions experts in World War II. For every box, designed to hold twenty-five muskets, the Government paid him two dollars and fifty cents. He had worked out a system of cost accounting adequate for a new business. Every component, every process, carried its own dollar-and-cents cost. When he delivered the first five hundred muskets, he was able to reduce his indebtedness to the Government by seventeen hundred dollars. The sum he still owed might have frightened a lesser man. Whitney was undaunted. And Jefferson believed in him.

This was the moment, just as everything had taken a propitious turn in the arms-making enterprise, that Phineas Miller begged Whitney to depart at once for South Carolina to persuade the legislature to purchase rights to the gin. Whitney's perturbation sounded in a letter to Stebbins. "I am literally in the predicament of the Old Woman who had so much to do, that she knew not what to do first. I am a perfect Ass between two bundles of hay — or rather I am surrounded with five or six hundred bundles all of which attract and *repell* equally. I can't attend to *this* thing because *that* thing requires my attention more. . . . I go on in a circle till I arrive at the point where I started." The shop ran well when he gave it his personal attention; if he were to be away for months, he feared the undoing of much of the progress he had made; he had frequently declared that he had to supervise his workmen constantly. In view of the past, would the United States Government tolerate further delay? Yet were he to refuse to go South, Miller & Whitney would probably lose the sale to South Carolina. Furthermore, he felt his personal honor at stake. He chose to risk the musket contract, in order to rescue the ginning business and redeem his name in the cotton country.

On his way to Columbia, the inventor and manufacturer stopped in Washington. Interviews with Jefferson set his mind at rest about allowing this new interruption to work on the muskets. The President, indeed, went further, acting upon his earlier offer to write to Monroe of Whitney's qualifications as an arms maker:

Mr. Whitney is at the head of a considerable gun manufactory in Connecticut, and furnishes the United States with muskets, undoubtedly the best they receive. He has invented moulds and machines for making all the pieces of his locks so exactly equal, that take 100 locks to pieces and mingle their parts and the hundred locks may be put together as well by taking the first pieces which come to hand. This is of importance in repairing, because out of ten locks, e.g. disabled for the want of different pieces, 9 good locks may be put together without employing a smith. Leblanc, in France, had invented a similar process in 1788 & had extended it to the barrel, mounting & stock. . . . Mr. Whitney has not yet extended his improvement beyond the lock. I think it possible he might be engaged in our manufactory of Richmond, tho' I have not asked him the question.

Five months later, upon Whitney's return from South Carolina to Washington in the spring of 1802, he found Dearborn fully amenable to a plea for more time on the arms contract. Hope of completing ninety-five hundred muskets in the fifteen months remaining under the terms of the revised contract was dead. Dearborn, however, realized that Congress had appropriated far more money for cannon and small arms than the War Department had been able to spend. Of the four hundred thousand dollars appropriated in 1801, he had obligated only eighty-six thousand. Money did not matter. If leniency about dates would eventually bring results, Whitney must have the time extension he needed. The upshot was an agreement that he was to have another year, until April 1803, in which to deliver the next thirty-five hundred stands of arms, and until April 1805 in which to complete the other six thousand.

Matters went well for the next six months — five hundred muskets completed in June 1802, in early September another five hundred, the latter supplied with brass pans, and the entire thousand packed in stout pine chests. "I am happy to find," wrote Whitney, "that this method of boxing promises to answer my expectations; the first parcel having been put up in the Boxes one year, are now in the same perfect order as when they were put up."

But again the affairs of Miller & Whitney took Whitney South, first to negotiate with the legislature of North Carolina and then to prepare the ground for reinstatement of South Carolina's purchase. Another five months lost to the shop at Mill Rock. He realized that similar interruptions were sure to recur during the remaining five years of the life of his patent, unless once and for all Southern cotton growers were to honor his rights. Nothing seemed likely to bring that to pass. He must again appeal for revisions to his Government contract. Dearborn acquiesced. On February 28, 1803, the two men signed a memorandum: "In case Eli Whitney shall deliver on or before the first day of May next, 500 Muskets in addition to those already delivered . . . then the said Whitney shall be allowed the privilege of delivering two thousand stands annually, the terms of the Contract notwithstanding."

Whitney's problems were not over, but thereafter his deliveries went forward regularly. He finished 500 stands in March 1803, another 1000 between July and October, only 1000 in 1804 and 1000 in 1805 — when building gins for North and South Carolina distracted his attention — but 1500 in 1805, 2000 in 1807, and the last 1500 between February 1808 and January 1809. Although he had stated in 1801 that he could not introduce brass pans on the first 1500 muskets, he bettered his word, for the arms he delivered in March 1803 carried that improvement. The 8000 of later make, priced at $13.50 apiece, embodied all the alterations he had suggested.

Until the summer of 1808, the War Department accepted each lot with enthusiastic approval; General Dearborn pronounced the arms "perfectly executed." Suddenly the Secretary of War touched off an explosion: "A circumstance occurred today which was mortifying and extremely unpleasant," he wrote Whitney on June 8. In a "conversation with a Gentleman relative to a contract for manufacturing 10,000 muskets, I mentioned your muskets as the only ones I had seen, made by contract that were faithfully executed." When Dearborn proudly displayed a sample, the would-be contractor who had expressed curiosity about these much-admired arms pointed out that the pan was not set close to the barrel, the breech plate was inferior, and he ". . . then drew the ramrod, which on trying its temper, was found as easily bent as any common Iron & destitute of any elasticity." Dearborn had hastily examined other samples of Whitney's work; they showed the same weaknesses. "These defects," the Secretary concluded, "are serious evils, and must occasion a new inspection of the Muskets received."

Whitney was disturbed, but he knew that his work was quite as good as that of others. He cited the case of his testing a ramrod made at Harpers Ferry which, though a specimen of the Armory's best workmanship, had broken into three pieces when Whitney sprung it gently. He had, moreover, heard the complaints of troops stationed in New Haven who were equipped with new muskets from the Springfield Armory and who found that most of the ramrods broke. Dearborn's papers of slightly later date bear out Whitney's contention. Of several thousand arms manufactured at the Springfield Armory three fourths were faulty, while the cocks and hammers produced by another private contractor were so brittle that they had broken when soldiers practiced with wooden flints. Government inspectors were as selective as possible. At the factory at Mill Rock the inspector tested the ramrods by throwing them forcibly down a musket barrel; any rod that did not ring he rejected as defective. Whitney argued that his workmen had no incentive to carelessness; he paid them by the day, not by the piece; he stated emphatically that the ramrods he had turned out were "equal to any which have ever been made in any part of the world." He was probably right. Expert workmanship could not overcome flaws in the iron, and no chemical or electrolytic process was then known by which to detect defects hidden from the eye. Government inspectors perforce continued to accept Whitney's muskets.

In January 1809, ten and a half years after entering into a contract with the United States Government, Whitney fulfilled his obligation. His cash profit totaled less than twenty-five hundred dollars, but his debts were paid, and the shop and its array of machine tools were now his. That property was valuable, but whether the tooling by then was far more elaborate than in 1801 when Philos Blake wrote of it is uncertain. Unquestionably in 1809 it did not include a milling machine, a lathe for shaping the black walnut blanks into stocks, or one for turning barrels — although, as Whitney later averred, he had already invented a barrel-turning machine that he decided not to install. His first milling machine and Thomas Blanchard's stocking lathe would not appear for another decade, and the automatic profilers and broaches which would later simplify manufacture of exact metal parts were still unknown in America.

Jefferson in 1801, while impressed with Whitney's achievements, noted that Leblanc, the gifted French arms maker, had carried interchangeability further than Whitney. Pursuing principles recognized by royal gunsmiths decades earlier, in 1788 the Frenchman had extended interchangeability "to the barrel, mounting and stock," whereas the American used the system only for the lock. Yet after the death of "Sieur Blanc," the methods he had used in the royal factory at Roanne fell into some disrepute. Although officials of the Republic introduced them in 1801

at the "Manufacture de Versailles," inspectors became increasingly critical of the quality of the muskets made by
machines. Perhaps wear reduced the accuracy of the cutting tools and the molds; workmen operating the machines may have grown careless. By 1806 an official report
stated, "As for the perfect uniformity upon which Roanne
established the reputation of its breech mechanisms, it is
an illusion." The percentage of defective work led the officer reporting to recommend hand fabrication of at least
part of the supply of small arms. The number of artisans
in France, many of them wedded to their ancient hand
skills, gave the nation an alternative the United States
lacked.

While in America, as in France, perfect interchangeability was an ideal never reached, here mechanized production had advantages that overrode obstacles. Whitney's
opportunity was his country's desperate need. He developed his machine tools independently, just as in England
Bentham and Brunel, without knowledge of Leblanc's innovations, evolved an interchangeable system for making
wooden pulley blocks for the British Navy. In fact, without
Jefferson's explicit testimony, Americans, somewhat like
Russian "scientists," prone to believe their country first in
all significant scientific or industrial development, might
doubt that France in the eighteenth century had had an
alternative to hand-fabricated, individually fashioned weapons, that Leblanc had anticipated Whitney in mecha-
nizing the manufacture of arms. Conversations with Jefferson may have heightened Whitney's awareness that for
the United States, where labor was scarce, machines, not

men, must become the backbone of production. Jefferson's encouragement and support of his plans unquestionably strengthened the influence Whitney exerted on American manufacturing methods. For, unlike many of Leblanc's compatriots, Whitney's countrymen quickly recognized the value of his work; in the United States it set the pattern for the future. Circumstances gave Whitney's achievements immediate and lasting importance.

One question remains: why a man of Whitney's inventive genius made such slight use of his authority to suggest improvements in American arms. Certainly he possessed the talent required to design a breech-loading rifle. John Hall received a patent in 1811 for a weapon of that general description, and by 1820 Hall, using Whitney's techniques of interchangeable manufacture, was turning out his rifles at Harpers Ferry. Whitney knew well the difficulties of producing the musket, if only because, as he himself later wrote, "the conformation of most of its parts corresponds with no regular geometric figure." Could he have failed to perceive also its shortcomings as a firearm? Had he given serious thought to the problem of designing a shoulder arm more suitable for the use of troops, it is hard to believe that he would not have succeeded. The reasons for his not attempting that service to his country are not far to seek.

First of all, he lacked leisure in which to consider the problem; he could not devote to it careful thought as long as the fight for the cotton gin continued. From the fall of 1801 until the patent expired six years later, he had frequent trips to make to South Carolina and Georgia, and, after Miller's death in December 1803, the surviving partner had the added burden of arranging all the details of carrying on the business of Miller & Whitney. During that period he engaged the competent mechanic, Roswell Lee, later superintendent of the Springfield Armory, to maintain the gins purchased by men of influence in the Southern states. Judge Johnson's decision came in December 1806, and Whitney still had to push through the lawsuits to recover from trespassers in Georgia. In 1808 he spent futile effort in trying to persuade Congress to extend the life of his patent. Time that he might have spent in designing an efficient new weapon went into defeating his foes in the South.

A weightier reason, and one that held long after the patent on the cotton gin was a cause lost to its inventor, was the matter of costs. The meagerness of Whitney's profit on the ten thousand muskets completed in 1809 made that factor all-important. No one of his era was so familiar as he with the costs of tooling. Retooling, then as now, could be still more expensive and, in the absence of a specialized machine tool industry, could be disastrously time-consuming. He would have had to discard machines otherwise still usable or at least make extensive modifications and corresponding changes in processing. In the first decades of the nineteenth century few men could grasp the scope of that task. Whitney could have anticipated protracted sessions in Washington, arguing his point, convincing or perhaps failing to convince one official after another, and the threat always present that political turnover would upset his arrangements as quickly as made.

As a man with his living to make and without reserves of capital, he would naturally propose only minor changes in the article he was manufacturing once he had his shop well equipped.

In 1853, the Secretary of War, Jefferson Davis, summed up the situation of the private contractor making weapons for the Government. The arms makers' lobby, by then impressively strong, had been urging the economy of closing down the Federal armories and leaving private companies to supply all munitions to the Government. Requested by Congress to state his views, Davis put his finger unerringly upon the weak spot of the plan:

Whilst the interest and professional reputation of an officer of the army in charge of a national armory would impel him to introduce all improvements, his military associations would lead him to learn, and his military experience teach him, the value of new modifications, made either in his own or other countries. On the other hand, the interest of the private contractor would be to reproduce indefinitely the model originally furnished to him; because every change would require either the abandonment of his tools, machinery &c., or a modification to adapt them to the manufacture of the improved model. For this reason, and also because his workmen would be less expert upon a new modification than upon a form to which they were accustomed, every change would be to the contractor an evil in which he would see increased trouble and diminished profit.

That on the eve of the Civil War the army itself fell victim to the fear of the time and cost of retooling supports the central thesis. When the Ordnance Department chose to cling to the muzzle-loader, instead of endangering the output of the Springfield Armory by converting to

the breech-loader believed ready to go into production,
the decision marked a sacrifice of quality to quantity, even
though the profit motive did not enter in. Problems of retooling and the concomitant question of quality versus
quantity similarly affected selection of weapons in World
War II.

For Whitney in the early years of the century retooling would have been more than a matter of profits. When
General Dearborn agreed in February 1803 to allow him
to turn out the muskets, with the minor alterations
specified, at the rate of two thousand a year, the contractor
had every reason to believe that he had won all the
favors he could expect. To propose changes so radical
that further delay must inevitably ensue would be to en-
danger the concessions he had but recently secured and
perhaps to imperil his future. Wolcott's letter of July 1799,
written, to be sure, before Whitney had proved the soundness of his methods, had represented the latent doubts
felt even by the men who had supported him strongly.
Too much postponement might revive those doubts, particularly were Jefferson to fail of re-election and a less
knowledgeable man than Dearborn to take office as Secretary of War.

Finally, and most important, all evidence points to
Whitney's greater interest in his system of manufacture
than in the specific article he produced. The pressure of
his debts had originally plunged him into the enterprise;
once launched upon it, he was caught up by the excitement of carrying it out and then of extending his scheme.
He might have manufactured, say, clocks or steam engines

with the same skill and enthusiasm that went into his muskets, if he could have obtained the credit he needed and felt assured of a steady market for his output at a price that would pay. He was, in short, only incidentally an arms maker. Other than to make his place in the world, his first concern was to develop machine tools. He would consequently avoid taking any step that could threaten the acceptance in America of his interchangeable system. Before he completed his first Government contract he dared not risk further revolutionary proposals; and in 1808, before he had finished the last of the ten thousand muskets, he found himself facing a new situation.

The long-term significance of his work was, indeed, not a well-made musket but a new approach to manufacturing. Certainly the United States needed shoulder arms — and in far greater numbers than the handful of American gunsmiths could have made by hand in years. Moreover, as Jefferson had noted, the greater uniformity of the parts of Whitney's machine-made guns, while still very imperfect, greatly simplified the problem of maintenance of arms in the field. But, vital though equipping the army was, ultimately more valuable was the marking-out of the path to American industrial might. Whitney's dedication to processes produced a weapon more powerful in strengthening the nation than any firearm could have been.

V I I

The Struggle for
Widespread Acceptance

OTHER MEN besides Whitney had faith in his
methods, but in the first years of the nineteenth century
the system had not yet won general endorsement. Doubts
about the utility of so novel a concept persisted long after
Whitney had proved it feasible. To establish his process firmly in America was a major preoccupation of his
later life.

Meanwhile the year 1808 brought an unforeseen crisis
to the manufactory at Mill Rock. Over the head of its owner
hung the fear of having to close it down altogether or
to find some entirely new article to make which people
needed in quantity and would pay well to get. Either
choice might be ruinous. The investment in tools
adapted primarily to arms manufacture put Whitney at
peculiar disadvantage. Conversion of a shop was a term
still unknown in a world where most men turned out their
products by familiar hand methods. At the first of the
year, he still had fifteen hundred stands of arms to deliver
on the contract of 1798. And he hoped that the War De-

partment would negotiate another contract as soon as he finished the first. He had, in fact, been putting out feelers since the summer of 1807. Now in the spring of 1808 a double blow awaited him in Washington. He had journeyed to the capital to present to Congress his petition for renewal of his patent on the gin and at the same time to secure from the Secretary of War a second contract for muskets. Not only did Congress adjourn without acting in his behalf, but his overtures to the War Department fell on deaf ears.

Past experience may have prepared him for the inaction of Congress; nothing could reconcile him to the attitude of the War Department. He knew that his reputation as a manufacturer stood high — no one had as yet found fault with his work — and he had had every reason to believe that officials respected his judgment. In 1803 General Dearborn had requested him to inspect possible sites for the waterworks at an installation the Government was planning to establish in South Carolina. In December 1806, Dearborn had invited him to take charge of the national armory at Harpers Ferry; the first superintendent had died, and the Secretary of War had tried to persuade Whitney to transplant himself, his best workmen and special machine tools to the Government establishment. When Whitney, still occupied with lawsuits in Georgia, declined, Dearborn had instructed James Stubblefield, the man appointed to the superintendency, to spend some time at Whitney's factory to study his methods. Not many months later Dearborn had again approached him, this time to ask whether he would undertake to make four thousand cavalry swords and a like number of artillery sabers with hilts and scabbards. Whitney's reply had set forth succinctly the possible drawbacks: "I have no doubt of the practicability of manufacturing in this Country, Swords which would bear respectable comparison with the celebrated Blades of Toledo & Damascus," but he had explained the need of time to devise the necessary machinery and of a factory to house it, "and to indemnify the expense of such an establishment, it should be carried on for several years." On lesser matters also officials of the War Department had sought his advice. And now he could get neither suitable contract nor promises. As he wrote his brother Josiah, "I have wholly relinquished the idea that it will be possible for me to make any contract with the present Secretary of War."

From the standpoint of public interest, Whitney's indignation was groundless. Certainly it was misdirected at Dearborn, for with the two national armories turning out shoulder arms at the rate of nearly twenty thousand a year, Government policy would reasonably decree no further contracts with private manufacturers except at prices below costs at the Government establishments. Since Federal installations had no taxes to pay and then, as later, charged into costs neither interest on the investment, obsolescence nor insurance, no private concern could compete on these terms. Congress, furthermore, quickly made clear that, while the Federal Government needed no contract muskets for supply of the standing army, the states would have to arm the militia, and the Federal Government would appropriate money for that purpose. Congress was voting two hundred thousand dollars for the states at the very moment Whitney was venting his anger at Dearborn.

Though disappointment rendered his views one-sided, Whitney's frustration was quite understandable. He had assumed that, once his system had won official approval, his factory could run indefinitely on Government orders. He had built his business on Federal patronage. Where was he now to find customers whose demands would be steady and whose credit was sound? His conviction that personal enemies were behind his troubles emerged in a letter to Catherine Greene Miller in September 1808: "I have for the last Eight months been trifled with by certain persons whose elevated station ought to have placed them above such conduct. I have been held in a state of suspense & uncertainty which prevented making general arrangements & I have been obliged to have recourse to temporary expedients." While he should have been the first person to realize that national armories tooled for production of muskets could not readily make side arms, the Government contract placed in 1808 with Simeon North for manufacture of pistols perhaps added to Whitney's sense of grievance.

At the moment, money was not his pressing need. Only the year before he had collected two thousand dollars in damages from trespassers in Georgia, and payments on rights to the gin had continued to come in from North Carolina until the patent expired. Using part of the lump sum he had received from South Carolina in 1805, he had invested in some highly profitable commercial ventures arranged through the recently founded banking and brokerage house of Oliver Wolcott & Company of New York. Wolcott's wide banking connections and shrewd business sense enabled him to guide Whitney's investments unerringly; and both men, now close personal friends, both before and after 1808 joined in various trading ventures. The money Whitney made in the China trade alone would have kept him from want. But such speculations, however successful, were not enough to satisfy Whitney. Quite apart from any financial returns, the manufactory at Mill Rock was his life. To close it would be defeat.

Whitney, moreover, had to think of more than his own purse and wishes. Some fifty workmen employed in his shop depended upon him for a livelihood. Their familiarity with machines would in time open other jobs to them, as Whitney, to his wrath, was later to discover; but the plan he had outlined to Wolcott in 1798 and adhered to thereafter, relying upon men with "family connections and perhaps some little property to fix them to the place," decreased markedly the ease with which his workmen could move. For men with families he had built solid stone houses, and for the unmarried he ran a boardinghouse near the shop, with a housekeeper in charge to cook and to wash and mend clothing. In this first mill village in America he maintained a paternalistic regime, without, however, carrying his supervision to the extent prevailing later in some Connecticut factories where employers required of their working people weekly attendance at church. He himself lived in one of the farmhouses that had stood on the property when he bought it, and here he installed the dozen or more boys he employed as apprentices. A housekeeper, aided in the kitchen by one or sometimes two girls, had the trying job of cooking, baking, scrubbing, mending, tending fires, nursing any child who was ill, and even making clothes for the apprentices. Since at one time Whitney alluded to having a household of twenty, little wonder that the turnover of housekeepers was frequent. Whitney kept watch over every detail in his village. Though his workmen would probably have preferred less attention to their personal lives, he obviously deemed it his duty to consider their welfare as well as his own.

Whitney had taken on responsibility, moreover, for his sister Elizabeth's sons, first for Philos, then for Elihu, and still later for his namesake, Eli Whitney Blake. One after the other the small boys came to live with their bachelor uncle and to benefit from advantages he could provide. That for the young nephews the arrangement at first had its drawbacks in no way lessened the financial burden Whitney had assumed. Philos had no notion of what his future at Mill Rock would mean when he wrote to his sister in September 1801, soon after he came: "I have not ben to school Sence I hav ben here and I cannot read or write one Half as well as i did when i came heare to lieve and i do not wish to live heare." His and his brothers' homesickness and feeling that their uncle rarely made time to attend to their wants soon gave way to appreciation of the opportunities "Uncle" opened up to them. Educating and training three boys for more than ordinary careers took money in the early nineteenth century. In addition, Whitney contributed to the expenses of his sister Elizabeth's household in Westborough, particularly after their father's death in 1807. To have an assured income was only less important to the "master manufacturer" than to have his life's work at the factory endure.

Suddenly, in October 1808, his immediate anxieties vanished. Through the good offices of Oliver Wolcott in negotiating with Governor Daniel Tompkins, Whitney secured a contract to make two thousand muskets for the militia of the State of New York. The five hundred muskets still to be made for the Federal Government and this new order would keep the plant running for at least two years more. The price Governor Tompkins agreed to was satisfactory — thirteen dollars for each stand of arms — and contracts with other states might very well follow. During 1809 and much of 1810 Whitney watched over his shop.

Although the weaknesses of his ramrods continued to be a sore subject, he had the satisfaction of discovering that General Dearborn still trusted him, for shortly before he delivered the last five hundred arms to the War Department, the Secretary of War wrote: "I . . . will rely on your own Inspection believing that you will inspect the arms with Candor and Integrity." As Whitney had dared hope, in February 1810 he obtained a contract from the State of Connecticut for seven hundred muskets. That November he delivered the two thousand muskets for New

York State, despite the setback of a serious illness and the departure of several skilled workmen who were "enticed away to Springfield." Will power carried him through his illness. He finished the arms for Connecticut in May 1811, at once contracted to make seven hundred more, and delivered the second lot a year later, shortly before the United States declared war on Great Britain. Thus he tided over without direct support from the Federal Government.

But Whitney paid dearly. For years he had driven himself hard. The journeys South had been exhausting. Having abandoned travel by ship, presumably to avoid the miseries of seasickness, he had had to take horse and buggy over bad roads or no roads at all, through mud and dust, and with little comfort at the end of each day's journey. He had known intense mental harassment. He had scarcely tasted leisure. In the farmhouse at Mill Rock which he called home, the confusions of the household of youthful apprentices and small nephews left him scant quiet. Whatever the competence of the stream of housekeepers who came and went, they gave him no companionship. The wife that he longed for he had not yet found. As he had once written Stebbins, "I am an Old Bachelor, overwhelmed in business, . . . constantly resolved to marry without allowing myself leasure to take one step towards carrying that resolution into effect." Other than his brother Josiah, and Stebbins in distant Maine, he had no one to whom to unburden himself. He was, he said sadly, "a solitary being, without a companion and almost without a friend — employed in this smutty occupa-

tion of Vilean and living on plain fare in a humble cot
tage."

The pace he set himself affected his health. During the
fall and winter of 1810, illness incapacitated him. In December he wrote to Dr. Lemuel Kollock, an intimate friend
of Phineas and Catherine Greene Miller and a founder
of the Georgia Medical Society:

> I was attacked with so much severity as to confine me to the
> house and with symptoms so alarming as wholly to unman all
> my Resolution — and I entirely gave up the expectation of
> being able either to travel or attend to any business this win-
> ter. After a fortnight, however, I was in great measure relieved,
> flattered myself that I should regain my health and resumed
> my intentions of going to Georgia. But my intervals of convales-
> cence have continued only for short periods and I am now
> altogether unable to travel. My face is at this time so much
> swolen that you would not recognize it, but cramps in the
> stomach and breast are more painful and excite more appre-
> hension.

At a later date, the diagnosis might be stomach ulcers.
For fifteen years Whitney had lived under constant stress.
During the fifteen years that remained to him he would
never enjoy robust good health. Nervous tension and
overwork manifestly heightened, if they did not cause, his
bodily ailments. His medical history had a twentieth-
century ring; in more ways than one he was the first
modern American businessman.

He used his ill health and the "pressure of business" as
justification for rarely visiting his family in Westborough
and never, after 1807, returning to see Catherine Greene
Miller. His brother Josiah served as his emissary to his

relatives; in his relations with Catherine he could employ no delegate. Perhaps he dared not again come under the direct spell of that charming but demanding woman. Repeatedly she besought him to come and, while chiding him for neglecting to write more often, accepted his apologies with gentle grace: "For indeed my beloved Mr. Whitney, your interest is my interest — your health my health — your happiness my happiness." Repeatedly he promised to come as soon as his affairs were in order. He set aside Dr. Kollock's warnings that Catherine was failing. In September 1814, Whitney would learn that he had waited too long; Catherine was dead, and the man whom she had set upon his career would discover that he had sacrificed to business the cherishing of a human relationship.

When, in May 1812, despite recurrent illness, Whitney completed the second lot of muskets for Connecticut, the uneasy peace between the United States and the great powers of Europe was approaching an end. In the years since 1798, doubts had periodically arisen in America about whether France or Great Britain were the foremost foe. By the summer of 1812, sentiment in Washington had crystallized. Great Britain held Canada on the Northern border, threatened the Western outposts, and subjected American ships on the high seas to humiliating search and American seamen to impressment. Napoleon, as many Americans realized, was equally ruthless and would probably give the United States even shorter shrift if he could. But in 1812, in the eyes of the "War Hawks" with influence in Congress, Britain, not France, had become the main enemy. On June 18, just as the ministry in London was dispatching conciliatory offers to America, the United States declared war.

Whitney's conservatism in every realm save mechanics and business management may have placed his sympathies with the anti-French groups. In 1802, after dining at a Washington tavern in the company of Tom Paine, he had expressed his loathing for the old Revolutionary. Like many of his contemporaries, and like Theodore Roosevelt a hundred years later who characterized Paine as "that dirty little atheist," Whitney despised "the putrid rattle snake which has died from the venom of his own bite." But the manufacturer always kept himself aloof from politics. If he shared the convictions voiced in parts of New England that the United States should make war, if at all, upon France, home of godless Jacobins and birthplace of "dangerous" ideas, he kept his views to himself. It mattered more to him that war had come than that President and Congress had chosen to fight Great Britain. What concerned Whitney was his country's need of weapons and his ability to help meet that need.

On June 29, in a letter to Madison's Secretary of War, William Eustis, he analyzed the problem. Great Britain herself, he explained, encountered difficulty in finding gunsmiths capable of making good musket locks. In the United States, where skilled workmen were far fewer, arms manufacture could not proceed "without the aid of a variety of heavy and expensive machinery, moved by water."

As waterworks are expensive and soon go to decay, the machinery should be so proportioned and the extent of each establishment such, as to keep *all* the machinery constantly employed. Any attempt to carry on such a manufactory without a solid, fixed and sufficient Capital must be abortive. The amount of the capital must be at least equal to double the value of the Arms delivered in one year — and this amount will not be sufficient unless the finished work be turned in and payment for the same received every ninety days. The establishment of such a manufactory . . . can in no case be accomplished in less than two years — and should be continued at least twenty years to warrant such an investment of capital.

Not only was his own shop "the most respectable" of the private arms factories in America, but the new methods he had invented were "practically useful and highly important to his country." He could not readily convert his machinery to other uses, and he hoped to continue fabricating muskets. He suggested that mutual benefits would result were the United States to award him a contract "upon such terms as to afford a fair prospect of a reasonable profit for his labor."

In 1809 and 1810, Tench Coxe, Purveyor of Public Supplies, had negotiated contracts with some nineteen gunsmiths for eighty-five thousand muskets at a price of ten dollars and seventy-five cents apiece. By the summer of 1812 the Government had received fewer than a third the number expected and, with the costs of manufacture rising, the Secretary of War concluded that many producers would default altogether. Whitney's offer, therefore, sounded attractive. Within three weeks a contract was signed. The manufacturer bound himself to deliver fifteen thousand muskets before the end of 1820. He was to follow the pattern of the arms he had made for New York State except that, since the "French barrel is rather too long for Convenience," he was to reduce the length of the barrel to forty inches. He was to start delivery before the first of May 1813, and thereafter complete yearly "not more than three thousand nor less than fifteen hundred." The United States was to advance money and make payment on the same basis as in the earlier contract with Whitney. The price set per musket was thirteen dollars. As formerly, Whitney must provide bond for "faithful performance."

Here was fresh triumph. Whitney again had won Federal patronage and under seemingly favorable conditions: the price assured profits, the time allowed was generous, and no retooling was necessary. So confident was he that all would go well that in October 1812 he contracted with Governor Tompkins for another two thousand muskets for New York State. And for nearly a year all did go well. Although the British blockade of the seacoast interfered with his obtaining supplies and he fell somewhat behind his production schedule, he felt no profound anxieties even when he failed to meet the May 1 delivery date for the first five hundred arms. He had learned, to be sure, from the master armorer at Springfield, that the new Commissary General of Purchases, Captain Callender Irvine, was displeased over Whitney's contract, since Irvine and Marine Wickham of the War Department's laboratory in Philadelphia hoped to foist their own model musket upon the United States Army. Whitney had also heard rumblings of the conflict between his friend Colonel Decius Wadsworth, chief of the newly created Ordnance Department, and the Commissary General, but, with the shop at

Mill Rock running smoothly, the manufacturer believed that his contract was safe.

The storm that broke over him at the end of June 1813 originated in the ideas and fierce ambitions of Callender Irvine. Irvine wanted to see the War Department adopt the musket in which he had an interest, though it was a model with little to recommend it. Equally Irvine wanted personal power. While holding the post of Superintendent of Military Stores, he had doubtless convinced himself that Government procurement policies were basically unsound. His aim was to eliminate all contracts for arms, increase the number and size of the national armories, and then have one man made responsible for supervision and control of all ordnance production. He might be the man. Later generations of officials would periodically revive parts of his plan; each proposal in turn would die on the vine. Filled with pride of service, Irvine doubtless pictured himself in a key position effecting needed reforms. He may have firmly believed that his plan alone could bring about efficiency and economy in providing the nation with military equipment. In the internal conflict within the War Department during 1813 and 1814, principles became confused with personal intrigue. But the most generous interpretation of Irvine's motives cannot condone the ruthlessness of the methods he used. Whitney came to be one of his main targets because of the fame of the factory at Mill Rock and the prestige of its owner.

In a series of skillful attacks upon the work of men who had accepted contracts for small arms in 1809 and 1810, Irvine had discredited Tench Coxe, who had placed the contracts; Coxe's head rolled in the spring of 1812. Having taken over the duties of the Purveyor of Public Supplies in August 1812 when he was appointed Commissary General, Irvine next sought to secure the support of the Ordnance Department in his fight to dispense with contractors. Decius Wadsworth, first "Colonel of Ordnance," was opposed. Irvine's campaign then began to smack of intimidation; it gained strength after January 1813 because the new Secretary of War, General John Armstrong, tended to take Irvine's statements at face value. The Commissary General directed his fire at the Springfield Armory: the armories were a responsibility of the Colonel of Ordnance. Inspectors under Irvine's influence reported the muskets made at Springfield defective. Wadsworth fought back, echoing the opinion of Tench Coxe that the character of inspectors might determine the character of the work they accepted. Concluding apparently that the Ordnance Department could wait to be brought into line, the Commissary General reverted to direct attack upon the contracting system. He either willfully forgot or did not know of the determined efforts of officials in the 1790's to persuade manufacturers to risk the hazards of making arms for the Government.

"What cost the Govt. about 60,000$," he wrote Armstrong, "not one arm of the whole is fit for service, or worth one cent but what they may bring as old iron or brass at auction." In his letters, the contractors — many of whom had borne heavy financial losses in attempting to meet the Government's requirements — all appeared to be unscrupulous self-seekers:

These private contracts are exceptionable in many ways and every respect. Better to increase the number of our public establishments and the number of hands at those already in operation and bring the whole under the superintendence of one judicious and independent man . . . It will be safer for the Govt. to expend two or three hundred thousand dollars on building armories than to advance so much money to individuals who will expend it in erecting buildings and machinery for themselves and disappoint the Govt. as to a supply of arms confidently calculated to be received within the period specified in their contracts.

That statement outlined Irvine's strategy in clearing Whitney from his path. As long as the master manufacturer was making weapons for the army, the contract system would stand. In late June, 1813, the Commissary General informed the Secretary of War:

Mr. Eli Whitney . . . has not delivered a single musket, tho' he should have delivered on or before the 1st of May last, at least 500 muskets. When the engagements of these contractors are not complied with as to time, I recommend that the contracts shall be cancelled. I have written today to Mr. Whitney stating that I have a general authority of that kind and that I will most assuredly exercise it. The Govt. has been trifled with long enough, in all conscience, by these contractors.

The "Artist of his Country," while aware of the hostility such a letter revealed, put faith in a personal interview with Irvine. It was useless. That fall, Irvine, instead of forwarding the five-thousand-dollars advance then due, listed the defects in Whitney's muskets: "The bayonet is two inches too short . . . the lower part of the butt is too long . . . the barrel is very crooked, and the britch is not water tight . . . the main spring is very indifferent, and the toe of the hammer too sharp . . . These defects must be remedied, or the Muskets will not be received or paid for by me."

Point by point, Whitney answered the charges, explaining that he was following the model former Secretary of War Eustis had selected. The proper length of a bayonet was a matter of opinion: "Agreeable to the Standard length of a French Bayonet, which is about 14 inches, the Bayonet in question is too long. Some have supposed that a Bayonet ought to be *thirty inches* long. And several thousand have been made of that length." He announced his willingness to make modifications if the Government would meet the cost, but neither party to a contract could legally force changes unacceptable to the other. Irvine's reply was disdainful. "I did not point out the exceptions to your musket with a view to consult your opinion, which would have been improper for two very obvious reasons. First you are not a practical Gun Smith, as I have been informed, and again, you are too deeply interested in the matter. . . . You have failed to execute your engagements. . . . It is therefore my duty to require of you to refund promptly, the money with interest, which has been advanced to you by the United States, which I now do."

The feud for months remained a battle of words. Whitney, again stricken with illness — rheumatism, his brother declared — had little taste for the fray, but he felt that if he were to survive as an arms maker he must not give an inch. He reminded his opponent that he could not arbitrarily cancel the contract, and as for the slur upon the manufacturer's capabilities:

I can, with my own hands, in the first place make my tools and then from the raw materials make a musket with as much precision, exactness, and finished workmanship as belongs to any Musket which I have ever seen — and I have seen and examined with attention the muskets made both in this Country and the principal Countries of Europe. . . . I am indebted to no man for planning or executing any part of my Machinery. I have always directed in person the intire detail of the business both as to the forms and modes of working. The more difficult branches I have executed myself. After having pursued the business for fifteen years . . . my ignorance of the subject should be ascribed to a want of capacity rather than a want of experience!

Irvine, though reporting to the Secretary of War that "we are at loggerheads" and reiterating his belief that the Government should cancel the contract, bided his time in hopes that Congress would pass a bill placing under a single superintendent all contractors and the Federal armories and arsenals as well. The bill failed in the Senate. The Commissary General had to take a new tack.

Irvine, while working on General Armstrong to declare Whitney's contract defaulted, persisted in withholding the promised advances of money and, still more disrupting to the manufacturer's work, ignored every request that he send an inspector to prove the finished musket barrels. Whitney protested both measures. The delay in inspection was an even more forceful bludgeon than the denial of funds. Barrels ready for test in November 1813 were still unproved and piled high at the factory six months later. The British, freed of the immediate threat of Napoleon, in the spring of 1814 were pouring troops into the United States, and still Whitney, through no fault of his own, could not deliver the muskets the United States Army needed. In desperation he went to Washington to present his case directly. In a formal memorandum to the Secretary of War, he described his efforts to hasten production. He had invested in "two new sets of water-works, one at Salisbury and the other at Haddam, for forging the Barrels"; nearly a thousand muskets were awaiting proof, and parts of two to three thousand more were "in great forwardness." He begged the Secretary to take the action necessary to permit the work to proceed. Armstrong, however, had listened to Irvine and was already setting machinery in motion to bring Government suit against the contractor.

At that moment Whitney appealed to the Secretary of State. James Monroe, recalling Jefferson's endorsement of Whitney's work, submitted the problem to the President. Madison himself then discussed it with Whitney. The affair was assuming mighty proportions. Armstrong became worried. When the harried Secretary of War took counsel with his chief of Ordnance, Wadsworth not only commended Whitney's work warmly but observed that many manufacturers in the United States had failed altogether in attempts to make arms. "The business is not yet so firmly established as to endure the incision-knife and caustic in curing its defects. Tampering and trying experiments with it will be premature and Hazardous until it takes firmer root." Armstrong evidently perceived that whatever merit lay in the plan of exclusively Government-owned armories, wartime was not the moment to follow it out; eradication of an infant industry at that point in American history could serve no public purpose. The outcome for Whitney was immediate payment of the five thousand dollars, by then eight months overdue, and an order from Armstrong to Irvine to send an inspector to New Haven.

Whitney, like the Colonel of Ordnance, knew that Irvine's next move would be to impose excessively stringent standards of inspection. But what was standard? The argument about the length of the bayonet was merely one example of the uncertainty of specifications consisting of a sample musket to copy. Since measuring instruments were far from precise, gauging, when used at all, was primitive. Producers in fact used no gauges in the course of manufacture, and inspectors usually gauged and tested only finished weapons. Chemical formulae for powder were also inexact. Powder supposedly uniform varied from one lot to another. Colonel Wadsworth, realizing that the Springfield Armory would suffer along with Whitney if inspectors assigned to New England were to use stronger powder charges than official regulations called for, repeated to Whitney the specifications established by the Secretary of War in 1798, based on French standards. Recently, wrote Wadsworth, Irvine's men had been substituting proof powder conforming to British specifications. This augured ill: too strong a charge could burst any barrel.

In mid-August, when Marine Wickham and an assistant arrived in New Haven to comply with the official order to inspect Whitney's muskets, they brought with them proof powder "of approved strength." "Approved strength" might mean anything Irvine chose. The crisis had come. Whitney hurriedly wrote Colonel Wadsworth:

If you can prevail upon the Secretary to fix upon a fair proper and uniform mode of proving musket barrels, you will render the public a great service and relieve me and many others from the most vexatious and ruinous embarrassment. . . . Immediate and great exersions will be made to induce the Secretary of War to establish a proof which has been improperly presented by subordinate officers of the Government. . . . I wish for nothing but that which [is] fair and proper.

Four days of angry exchange between Whitney and Wickham ended in the departure of the inspectors without looking at the muskets.

Whitney's fury was all-consuming. He described Wickham as a man "under the strong bias of prejudice and passion." Then, controlling his rage, the manufacturer set down for the Secretary of War a detailed account of the fundamental disagreements between inspector and producer. When he had inquired of Wickham what "Principles and Rules" were to govern the proving, the inspector "appeared to be averse to a free communication." He admitted to having come with explicit instructions, but he refused to allow Whitney to see them. Yet these would determine final judgments. "I can never while I retain my senses," wrote the outraged contractor, "under any circumstances, consent to be bound by an instrument, to which I am not a party — which I have never seen — and which I must never be permitted to see." He again asked the Secretary to send a competent, fair-minded inspector to test the finished muskets and added a note of warning: British raiders along the Sound might any day capture the guns.

A few days later Whitney took matters into his own hands. He explained to Armstrong the necessity of keeping manufacturing processes moving in an orderly fashion. Musket barrels should be proved as soon as they had been bored to the right caliber, cut to the specified length, ground to avoid excess weight, and breeched. To test them at a later stage of manufacture was wasteful of time. Months had gone by, and now he was unwilling to wait longer. He had engaged James Carrington, the man who had passed upon most of the arms of Whitney's first contract, to prove this first lot of the second. Since Carrington was not now employed by the Government, Whitney would raise no objections to a second, more official inspection, but, as the delay was not his, he would refuse to pay the five hundred dollars a second testing would cost. Though Whitney never knew it, one of Armstrong's last official acts was to heed the contractor's plea. He bypassed Irvine by directing Major Bomford, Assistant Commissary General of Ordnance, to send a reliable man to examine Whitney's muskets; since they had already been proved once, the inspection should be limited to testing a hundred selected at random from the thousand completed. Unwittingly, Armstrong anticipated a procedure first formally adopted during World War II, a procedure whereby statistical methods of quality control based upon a sampling technique superseded inspection of every finished piece. But Armstrong's order never went into effect.

Swift-moving events in the war with Great Britain suddenly blotted out the internal war. At the end of August

1814, redcoats captured Washington, burned the Capitol and the Executive Mansion and, seemingly with no opposition, prepared to overrun the rest of the country. Public humiliation and anger swept away thought of all else. The demoralized Armstrong retired. Monroe became Secretary of War. All officials at this critical moment recognized the importance of every arms factory in America, Whitney's and the national armories above all. When the enemy took the revenue cutter assigned to protect New Haven, fear of losing the manufactory at Mill Rock became acute. Although the War Department dispatched an artillery officer to install a shore battery, Whitney dared not trust to its force. He sold the thousand finished muskets to Governor Tompkins of New York. New York State paid for proving and shipping the much-wrangled-over guns.

In February 1815, with the peace treaty signed in Ghent, Congress took steps to clarify the duties of various branches of the War Department. Public law placed the Ordnance Department in charge of all contracts for arms and of the Federal armories. The act blasted Irvine's hopes. But Whitney still felt uneasy. Alexander Dallas, who had succeeded Monroe as Secretary of War, agreed to continue the contract but left it under Irvine's control. In the spring, Whitney wrote a letter direct to President Madison, enclosing the entire file of correspondence with Irvine and requesting that some other officer or other government agency handle the contract. The result was the transfer of inspection of Whitney's output to the Ordnance Department and in 1816 assignment to that agency of inspection of all contract arms. To Whitney's great satisfaction, James Carrington became the official inspector at the Mill Rock manufactory.

The intensity of the personal feud between Irvine and Whitney obscures the underlying conflict of principle. If, in time, hatred of Whitney beclouded Irvine's vision of his primary plan, he seems at first to have seen in the manufacturer the exponent of a system that ran counter to public interest, a man therefore to control or destroy. Whitney viewed Irvine as a nefarious conspirator intent solely on self-aggrandizement. Yet a larger issue was there.

Before 1815 many features of public administration had not yet jelled. Beyond the Post Office and the Mint, it was not clear what economic activities should be under public ownership. On the one hand, individualists in the early years of the Republic feared that a Government monopoly of arms manufacture might lead to a kind of dictatorship. On the other hand, taxpayers were reluctant to swallow Government patronage of individual firms which gained their experience at public expense. The opponents of "creeping socialism" and the advocates of a Government-controlled economy still carry on the debate. The course Congress and the President chose in 1815 resolved the problem of procuring munitions in a fashion that, by and large, still obtains. The War Department continued to let contracts for arms to private manufacturers, the Federal armories gradually expanded, and the Ordnance Department supervised the production of both sources of supply.

The new arrangement suited Whitney perfectly. His

dealings with the Ordnance Department had been friendly
since its inception in the summer of 1812, and Colonel
Wadsworth, who on occasion had signed a personal letter
to Whitney *Affectionately Yrs,* accorded him fair treatment. He would receive payment for his work promptly,
get an honest appraisal of its quality and, with the war
over, be subject to no extreme pressures to meet delivery
dates exactly. Wadsworth, moreover, acting upon the rec-
ommendation of his friend, appointed Roswell Lee to the
superintendency of the Springfield Armory. With Lee, once
an employee of Miller & Whitney and later a Lieutenant
Colonel in the army, Whitney knew he could work harmo-
niously. Co-operation with the national armories would
be helpful both to them and to him. He could now complete his contract in peace and, a matter still dearer to
his heart, freed of the heckling of Irvine, he could give
time and thought to designing new machine tools.

After May 1815, his business ran without hitches. In
June he made his first delivery on the contract of 1812,
a thousand muskets proved by Carrington and paid for by
the Government without quibbling. Work moved along
steadily, although, partly because the first lot of guns had
gone to New York State, and partly because some six hundred barrels burst in the proving, he would not complete
the contract until 1822.

In the meantime, he turned his attention to improving
his machines. He developed a way of increasing the efficiency of the trip hammers used in welding barrels, and,
in keeping with the generous spirit of give-and-take which
marked his relationship with the Ordnance Department,

he showed Lee at Springfield how to drive the hammers by belts rigged to a water wheel. Lee reported delightedly: "The trip hammers operate extremely well, the barrels now cost 30 cents less. The hammers can give 400 blows a minute." Whitney also offered the armory the design of a barrel-turning machine he had invented as early as 1808 but never built. "I would put it into operation," he wrote Lee in 1818, "if I could see any prospect of a fair remuneration for the invention & expence & risque of the Experiment. But the probability is that some person would contract to make the barrels & not only take advantage of my invention but intice away the workmen whom I had instructed in the use of the Machine before I could be half compensated for the expence of making it." Only where new devices added to the efficiency of his shop without threatening his hard-won security did he put them to work.

He had apparently had one all-important innovation in mind when the battle with Irvine distracted his attention. A number of the fifty components of the Charleville musket, before 1822 the model still standard for the United States Army, had such irregular contours that use of filing jigs and fixtures could not prevent bottlenecks in production. If he could build a power-driven machine capable of cutting those parts automatically, he could turn out work faster, more cheaply and with far greater accuracy than was possible otherwise. A skilled French mechanic, Jacques de Vaucanson, had used a mechanized rotary file in the early 1780's, but Whitney, had he known of it, would not have found it right for the job he wanted to do. He needed

not a grinder but a mechanized cutter. Some time before
the end of 1818 — the precise date is unknown — he built
his first milling machine.

A milling machine is today basic equipment in any
shop where operations include the shaping of exact metal
parts. In 1818 the introduction of this ingenious machine
tool was a revolutionary technological advance. Simeon
North, his descendants declared a century later, was using some kind of miller as early as 1808, but few people
saw it, and it consequently had no important influence
upon later machine tool design. Whitney's, on the other
hand, came quickly into wide use. In his machine a
"chuck" or vise held the work to be shaped upon a plate
moved by a power-fed screw driven by a worm gear; the
cutting tool, rotating on its own axis and positioned to remove the metal, chip by chip, to a calibrated depth, had a
cutting edge irregularly shaped to correspond to the contours the component required. The miller could thus rapidly turn out pieces of intricate form. In some respects, the
man who invented the miller in 1818 was a greater benefactor to his country than the inventor of the cotton gin
itself. Whitney at once put the fruits of his genius at the
disposal of the Federal armories. Lee soon had in operation at Springfield milling machines modeled on Whitney's. The inventor took justifiable pride in pointing out
to John C. Calhoun, a fellow Yale alumnus then Secretary
of War, the advantages the new methods offered in musket manufacture. Whitney's letter, written in 1823, spoke
not only of his milling machine but also of the die forging
he had introduced in making the trigger guards. These in-

novations, he announced, produced work "with more expedition & accuracy" than hand filing could provide.

The postwar decade was an "era of good feeling" between the War Department and Whitney more genuine than that among political leaders. Lee at the Springfield Armory and Whitney at Mill Rock worked closely together in establishing wage rates, in giving each other "black lists" of undesirable employees, in purchasing foreign supplies, especially steel, and in attempting to control the price of iron. When the Salisbury ores showed signs of deterioration, the two men took counsel together about other possible sources. The extensive correspondence month after month contained innumerable discussions of manufacturing techniques. With men at Harpers Ferry Whitney's exchanges were less voluminous but equally amicable. He journeyed to the Southern armory to see John Hall's processes for making his breech-loading rifle but in actuality saw only part of the works. Wadsworth, to the day of his death in 1821, frequently consulted with Whitney on that touchy question of uniform standards of manufacture and inspection, or about the design for a new model musket. When George Bomford, a competent engineer and a designer of cannon, succeeded Wadsworth, the cordiality between the Ordnance Department and Whitney remained unimpaired.

Influenced perhaps by this mutual good feeling, Whitney believed he had won the battle to establish the interchangeable system in arms manufacture. A letter to Calhoun, President Monroe's Secretary of War, in 1821 summarized the progress of acceptance as Whitney then saw it:

> So strong are the prejudices of Education & force of habit that although several of the Machines & many of the improved modes of working, invented by your Memorialist had from time to time been introduced into the public Armories, it was not until he had demonstrated the superiority of his System by a successful and uninterrupted experiment of ten years continuance, that it was adopted into the Public Armories. Since that period the quality . . . has been greatly improved without increasing the expence.

Possibly it was because his work achieved a degree of uniformity other armories could rarely maintain that he failed to realize the extent of doubts about the method which lingered in the minds of many well-informed men. In June 1819 his good friend Roswell Lee had written to another able Massachusetts arms maker:

> I can only inform you that my instructions are to make the muskets with that exact uniformity, that the several component parts will fit one musket as well as any other. Relative to the *practicability* of this course, experience must decide. With regard to the *utility* of the measure to the extent required by Government, the fidelity as well as the respect due to the authority from which I receive instructions . . . forbid me to express an unfavorable opinion . . . except when in my opinion the public interest makes it an indispensable duty. . . . My impressions are, that this mode [of uniformity within the musket] must be entered into and pursued until experience (which is the most sure test) proves its practicability and utility, or the reverse.

Another officer at Springfield pointed out that "to attain this grand object of uniformity of parts," only one procedure was feasible, "viz: making each part to fit a standard gauge." Lacking standard gauges, most contractors ran into trouble. Wholehearted acceptance of the interchangeable method would not come in Whitney's lifetime.

Whatever uncertainties they felt about the economy of the "uniformity system," by 1820 arms makers and public officials were recognizing Whitney's stature as an engineer and an industrialist, though neither term had as yet grown familiar in America. While supervising work on the musket contract and installing his milling machine in his shop, he had built an elaborate chemical apparatus for Professor Silliman of Yale and made for Oliver Wolcott patterns for a new cast-iron pump. In August 1822 he completed the second Government contract for arms and agreed to extend it by manufacturing three thousand more. Two weeks later he signed a third contract, this time to produce fifteen thousand muskets of a new design. For, after several years of anxious debate, the Ordnance Department had settled upon the characteristics of the weapon to replace the modified Charleville model that dated back to 1777. Because the costs of fabrication were necessarily still undetermined, the price set for all contractors was twelve dollars a musket, but the Ordnance Office arranged a sliding scale. When a year's operation had shown what the average unit costs were at the Federal armories, the twelve dollar price might go up or down. For the first time, the War Department included in costs "the interest in the Entire Capital employed at the Armories, insurance against all risks, with the addition of such further percentage for wear and decay, as shall be sufficient to preserve the said Capital unimpaired." Whitney had at last carried his point that costs must include more than labor and raw materials. Contractors of a later time have frequently wished that these provisions for cost accounting had endured within the Ordnance Department. Beginning with January 1, 1824, Whitney was to deliver three thousand muskets yearly, and, according to announced policy, could count on another contract when he had fulfilled the current one satisfactorily.

Colonel Bomford, in justifying the policy of renewals, outlined the history of the contracting system:

In 1798, when the first attempt was made, there were but few persons in the country acquainted with the business; and but one of those (Mr. Whitney, of Connecticut,) who embarked in it succeeded; all the rest were either ruined by the attempt or found the business so unprofitable and hazardous as to induce them to relinquish it. In 1808 . . . a renewed attempt was made, and many of the contractors who were then engaged in the business have also failed. The steady support and patronage given by the Government since that time to the contractors, whose skill, perseverance, and capital saved them from early failure, has resulted in the firm establishment of several manufactories of arms, and preserved to the country establishments of great importance to its security and defence.

If Whitney wanted further vindication, he may have found it in the regulations promulgated in 1823 to guide the inspection of small arms. Powder would continue to vary in quality, but the Ordnance Department set such standards as it could. However faulty its specifications and testing procedures, it put limits upon the individual inspector's frailties and whims. In examining musket barrels, he was to "stretch a line through the barrel, and apply it to at least four sides of the bore, to ascertain if the interior is straight." He was to use "go" and "no go" gauges: "The small plug should pass freely through the barrel, and the large plug should not enter its whole length. If the barrel will not receive the small plug, or if it will admit the large plug, the barrel will be rejected." As far as measuring devices permitted, other gauges checked other components. Imposition of explicit standards improved the quality of arms and, although the Ordnance Department first supplied manufacturing gauges to contractors in the 1830's, the regulations assured private firms of the 1820's equitable treatment.

In the fall of 1822, the illness that proved fatal two and a half years later began to curtail Whitney's activities, but when pain was not wholly incapacitating him, in the last years of his life he could look back upon his achievements with pride. He had weathered adversity and, in staving off high-handed attack, had helped bring about a definition of standards as accurate and impersonal as rules could contrive. He had taught other manufacturers and the United States Government some principles of cost accounting. He had built, put to use, and shown others how to use new tools of production. By the work of his own hands, he had convinced influential Americans of the feasibility of interchangeable manufacture, and, if not everyone as yet felt sure of its value, the method would receive long, careful trial until proved. He had won the confidence and respect of national leaders and, perhaps equally gratifying to

a person of his special interests, mechanics and tool builders the country over looked up to him as the first of them
all. Yet he, like his professional associates, knew that he
had not worked alone. The development of machine tools
that offset the shortage of labor in America was bringing to
the United States its own industrial revolution. The
"American System" of arms manufacture in the 1850's
would invade and capture Europe. But these changes were
the work of many men, obscure as well as famous. Whitney, nevertheless, in the eyes of his contemporaries, stood
first among those who made the system effective.

V I I I

The Last Years and
Ultimate Achievements

BETWEEN 1794 and 1817 Whitney had no personal life. In 1794, warmed by the admiration important men had accorded his invention, he had enjoyed a few weeks in Catherine Greene's society at Mulberry Grove while he installed the first gins there. Returned to New Haven, he had again plunged into work in his shop. For nearly twenty-three years thereafter business problems had absorbed him, draining his energy and consuming the leisure he might otherwise have found. Men, to be sure, paid him honor: Yale awarded him a Master's degree, the Connecticut Academy of Arts and Sciences listed him as a charter member, the United States Military Philosophical Society admitted him to membership, and the state appointed him Justice of the Peace in Hamden. On occasions he dined with New Haven neighbors, with President and Mrs. Timothy Dwight of Yale College, with Elizur Goodrich and his family, or with other old friends. Probably he found brief companionship in Washington City, in his memorable conversations with Jefferson and short talks

with Madison. He obviously took pleasure in his relationship with Oliver Wolcott, however much their discussions
turned upon investments and profits. He managed to correspond with some regularity with Josiah Stebbins in
Maine; the sedate, literal-minded and affectionate Stebbins was the one person to whom he let himself pour out
his heart over the years. Letters kept him in touch with
his brother Josiah and his sister Elizabeth, as with his father before the older man's death, while the presence of
the young Blake nephews in the household at Mill Rock
was an added link with the family. His personal letters to
Georgia, and particularly to the widowed Catherine Miller,
grew fewer and fewer with the passage of time. Yet he
formed a friendship with Dr. Lemuel Kollock, originating
in gratitude to the physician for watching over Catherine
and expressed at one moment in the gift of a "Watch Engine," at another in acquiring for the doctor "a pair of
Full Blooded Spanish Merino Sheep."

But most of these contacts were intermittent or casual,
mere palliatives to his loneliness, often serving to under-
score the emptiness of all but his business life. He made
an abortive attempt in 1800 to have Phineas and Catherine
Miller arrange at long-distance a marriage for him with
a young woman in Georgia, probably one of Catherine's
two unmarried daughters. After that failure, he abandoned for nearly seventeen years any serious effort to establish a family and a real home for himself.

In early 1817 the bachelor existence he had constantly
deplored came to an end. If he wrote to his relatives and

friends of his impending marriage, the letters have disappeared. On January 6, 1817, he married Henrietta Edwards, daughter of his friend Pierpont Edwards; as a granddaughter of the famous eighteenth-century preacher and philosopher, Jonathan Edwards, she was a member of the old New England aristocracy. From the standpoint of social prestige, Whitney could hardly have done better. Henrietta was by then thirty-one, Whitney fifty-two. He must have known her since her childhood. Why he waited so long remained a secret, perhaps hidden from Henrietta herself. His behavior suggests that as long as Catherine Greene Miller was alive, deep emotional ties held him in unadmitted bondage. The surviving letters that passed between Catherine and Whitney contain nothing beyond mutual respect and affection, and yet stronger feeling seems to lurk behind the words. As if captivated and still fearful of her and her demands, he avoided seeing her but could not entirely break away. The presumptive evidence would be stronger had he married slightly earlier, for Catherine died in September 1814 and, although the struggle with Irvine occupied him for another nine months, his marriage took place a year and a half after he had resolved that problem.

About Henrietta's feelings the record is completely blank. Her brilliant father, repudiating the precepts of the stern background in which he had grown up, reportedly kept a "doxy" after the death of his wife when Henrietta was fourteen. A successful lawyer, a true intellectual like his father before him, charming but shockingly unconventional in the view of most of his Connecticut neighbors, Pierpont may well have been a trying parent for any young woman in that day, although the endless stream of distinguished men who sought his company must have had its attractions for the daughter of the house. Far from good-looking, Henrietta nevertheless may have longed desperately for what she perhaps feared she might never get — a home of her own where she could live out her life in respectable matrimony. At the age of thirty-one she stood in dreadful peril of dying a spinster. She may, on the other hand, have cherished an admiring devotion to Whitney from her girlhood onward. His wealth could now offer her a comfortable future, and his standing in New Haven a social position an Edwards could accept. Whatever her motives in marrying her father's contemporary and friend, she brought to her husband the loyalty and affection which he needed and wanted and which he gave in equal measure to her.

Of the few troubles that broke the contentment of the last years of his life, the first was the final settlement of the affairs of Miller & Whitney. Why he should have found the very prospect distressing in the spring of 1818 is a question probably only to be answered by reflecting upon the character of his relation with Miller and Catherine and upon the humiliations to which Southern cotton growers had subjected him. Though many successes had intervened to soften the memory of stinging disappointments and defeats, he was manifestly uncomfortable about the coming discussions, and miserable lest chance confront him with Russell Goodrich, Catherine's executor, Miller's intimate friend, and a former associate in the firm. These circumstances led Whitney to beg his nephew, Eli Whitney Blake, for help in affairs "which have been so numerous, embarrassing and oppressive that I am almost driven to delirium." Young Blake, graduated from Yale in 1816, would be a competent assistant. In July his uncle explained his anxieties more fully:

I am exceedingly pressed with other business . . . but if there is no other way I shall dismiss my workmen & relinquish all other business until this, with the Estate of Miller is settled . . . I have for many years been distressed by the situation in which I have stood relative to the Estate of Miller. A large amount will be claimed from me, which in equity & good conscience I ought not to pay — but now is the time & the best time to settle this business — & I would rather sacrifice three thousand Dollars than it should remain unsettled another year. Mr. G. . . . will be very impatient & is in many respects a difficult man to do business with; but on the whole it is vastly better for me to close it with him, than with any other person connected with Miller's Estate.

In response to this plea, Blake came that summer to take over some responsibility for the shop and to help his uncle prepare his statements for the referees who were to make the final distribution.

A considerable sum of money was involved. In 1814 Congress had chosen to reimburse the speculators in Yazoo land by awarding them eight million dollars for their original investment, variously estimated at somewhere between five hundred thousand and one and a half million dollars. Miller's estate had thus profited, whereas Whitney, then as earlier, contended that he had suffered incalculable losses from the damages done to the partnership. For this, the referees — his lawyer, Simeon Baldwin, and Goodrich's representative, Nathaniel Rossiter — allowed him fifteen thousand dollars, after they had conscientiously gone over all the tangled accounts. Each of the partners, one of them fifteen years dead, received eleven thousand and fifty-four dollars in cash. In light of the sums of money Whitney believed he might have made during the years he devoted to the gin and the ginning business, and considering the profits that would have accumulated had the courts in Georgia upheld his rights from the beginning or Congress extended the life of his patent, his feeling that Miller & Whitney had been a failure was sound. Six weeks after the settlement, Goodrich put the final period to the history of the firm in a letter to Whitney noting that "these things and these times have passed by; and other folks and other times, have succeeded."

A more personal trouble for Whitney was the sorrow of losing his youngest child in 1823. His happiness in having children was the greater for their having long been denied him. Frances Edwards, the oldest, was born in November 1817; a second daughter, named Elizabeth Fay for Whitney's mother, in 1819; and in January 1821 the hoped-for son and heir, Eli, Junior. The fourth child, Susan Edwards, died at the age of twenty-one months.

Meanwhile Whitney himself was fighting for his life. From 1820 onward, his steadily worsening health had caused Henrietta — and himself — some alarm. Although the temporary arrangement he had made with Eli Blake in the summer of 1818 became permanent, so that the younger man relieved him of much of the supervising of the shop, he continued to attend to many details in person. In the fall of 1820, while directing the rebuilding of the dam at the factory, he had been stricken with a severe attack of influenza that incapacitated him for some days. Subject to periodic illnesses for many years past, thereafter he never knew good health. Yet some months later, when he learned that Decius Wadsworth lay dying in Washington, Whitney had brought his old friend to New Haven where Whitney could visit him daily and ensure him good care in his last days. But the reserves of vitality upon which Whitney drew in protecting other people were already ebbing. In the fall of 1822, an enlargement of the prostate gland, a condition quite incurable in those days, threatened his life. It marked the beginning of the end that came twenty-eight months later.

Whitney's struggle to live was a measure of the inner man. The first dreadful attack began in September 1822 upon his return from Washington where he had been signing his third contract for muskets. For three weeks he suffered prolonged and repeated paroxysms of pain, "severe beyond description," a close friend reported. When at last these attacks subsided, weakness confined him to bed until late autumn. In November he was well enough to move about the house and to take pleasure in the society of neighbors and friends.

During this brief respite he enjoyed the peace and affection that enveloped him. Calls from distinguished men were frequent, among them his warm friend Professor Benjamin Silliman and Denison Olmsted, professor of Natural History at Yale and the inventor's first biographer. Whitney found relaxation in watching his children, delighting with them in their small pleasures, and endless amusement in observing his wife's tactics in her campaign to marry off Josiah. "Your sister Henrietta," he wrote his brother, "has lately taken the strange freak into her head of offering you to every Old Maid she sees — They all say yes — & thank'y too. I have no doubt that they will, every one of them, be greatly disappointed — & that she will get herself into a sad scrape." Two months later, pleasantries were forgotten; the attacks of shattering pain resumed. While family and friends despaired and the eminent physician in attendance declared medicine could do nothing, Whitney took steps to help himself.

He proceeded methodically to learn everything the doctor could tell him about his condition. Nathan Smith was one of the best trained and most learned physicians in America, a graduate of the Harvard Medical School who had studied abroad, launched the Dartmouth Medical School and the Department of Medicine at Bowdoin, and had come to New Haven in 1821 to organize a medical school at Yale and to teach anatomy, surgery, chemistry and clinical medicine. No one in the United States was better qualified to treat Whitney's case. Whitney, having listened to Dr. Smith's explanations, next read carefully every book he could borrow or buy which dealt with his disease. Professor Silliman, himself a scientist, marveled as he watched his stricken friend study the authoritative literature on the subject, inspecting the illustrative plates minutely and acting "rather as if he himself had been the physician than the patient." Silliman added: "Nothing he ever invented, not even the cotton gin, discovered a more perfect comprehension of the difficulties to be surmounted, or evinced more efficient ingenuity."

When he felt he had sufficiently mastered the problem, Whitney from his sickbed wrote to London and Paris for materials and with those constructed "instruments" that brought him immediate relief. With early-nineteenth-century squeamishness, contemporaries declared that "delicacy" forbade a description of these instruments, and few people saw them — but presumably they were a kind of flexible catheter, perhaps much like the one Benjamin Franklin had made in 1784. Torn with pain that Whitney himself likened to that caused by "the rack of the Inquisition," he succeeded in doing more for himself than the foremost medical man in the country had been able to do for him. Probably his inventive genius won him nearly two added years of life.

During part of the year 1823, after vanquishing the worst bouts of pain, and until the autumn of 1824, when new agony assailed him, Whitney again gave thought to his business. Since he and Henrietta had set up housekeeping in a rented house on Orange Street in New Haven, he delegated some responsibilities for the manufactory to his nephew Eli Blake, who in 1821 had established himself and his wife in Whitneyville, as the mill village had come to be known. But as far as his strength permitted, Whitney himself saw to the possible improvements in and about the shop. He had a road cut out of the live rock above his supply sheds, so that wagons driven up the hillside could dump their loads direct into the bins below and thus save him the cost of unloading by hand. He saw with satisfaction the construction of the lattice-truss covered wooden bridge across the Mill River at his plant. The hundred-foot span of bridge, the first built upon Ithiel Town's design, simple, sturdy and inexpensive, was the forerunner of the covered bridges that would soon span rivers and streams throughout New England. To Lee in Springfield, with whom he maintained some correspondence, he wrote in August 1824 of an innovation he had in mind for handling iron and steel. Explaining with a touching euphemism that his health was "very infirm," he spoke of an invention "for drawing, forging & fashioning Metals which is based on a principle entirely new & from which I have great expectations. If my life should be spared. . . . I shall test the principle by actual experiment in the course of the present year. If it answers my expectations it will form a new era in the business of forging Iron & Steel." He never made the experiment. He did, however, complete a drawing of a tumbler mill, the last design he ever made. The sketch is crude, but it shows that the inventor had perceived the feasibility of letting the friction caused by the knocking of small metal parts against each other wear off the rough edges of components. The tilting and rotation of the tumbling barrel filled with sand, oil, and the parts to be smoothed was a substitute for filing and grinding which machine shops still use.

By November 1824, Whitney's will power could no longer halt the advance of his malady, but his life dragged on amid untold suffering. Nearly two years before, Inspector Carrington had written Roswell Lee that Whitney, who had then been hovering near death, seemed "much more occupied with the cares and business of this world than with apprehensions respecting the future." In actuality, he had very real concern for the future, although not for his own place in the next world. He had been anxious to safeguard his family, and he was deeply troubled about the disposition of the shop. On November 22, 1824, he signed his will, making generous provision for Henrietta and the children; they were to have a large living allowance and, in lieu of the rented quarters on Orange Street, a six-thousand-dollar mansion of imposing proportions to be built on Elm Street. Each child was to receive, later, a share of their father's property; Elizabeth Whitney Blake was to have an annuity, and her children were to have cash bequests.

How to arrange for the continued running of the manufactory was more difficult; the contract for muskets must not lapse. James Carrington had become the foreman at Mill Rock, but he could not manage the financial end of the business. Even after Whitney had made his will, the problem of the shop distressed him; it seemed to penetrate his delirium and to disturb his hours of lucidity. Not until January 7, 1825, the day before his death, did he find a practical solution, which he embodied in a signed codicil to his will. Unless Eli and Philos Blake should refuse — an unthinkable contingency — they were to manage the business of making muskets until the contract was fulfilled. Each nephew, the codicil suggested, should have an annual wage of four hundred dollars, a yearly advance of five hundred dollars against profits, and two ninths of the final profits on the contract. It was an attractive proposal. Both younger men were intelligent — Eli, in fact, possessed of some of his uncle's inventive talent: he would contribute to the science of mechanics a study of the proper shape of gear teeth, and in 1858 he would invent a rock crusher for use in road building which, in essentials, was like the machines used today. Furthermore, both nephews were devoted to their uncle. He knew he could trust them to carry on his life's work.

Whitney's death brought sorrow to the community, for with happiness and prosperity he had mellowed. Always openhanded to his family, as he accumulated wealth he was generous to others also. At a time when a thousand dollars was a large sum of money, his estate showed seventy thousand dollars in personal notes for loans to individuals — people in trouble who, like himself in years past, could not borrow from banks or from commercial houses. Eminent men in New Haven had enjoyed his society. Although somewhat younger contemporaries had found him slow in conversation, the most critical had admitted that "his thoughts were clear and weighty," his ideas "exact and diversified." His friends had ranged from the arch democrat Pierpont Edwards to the stanch federalist Oliver Wolcott, for Whitney had avoided becoming what he once called a "polititioner" by refusing ever to make political judgments. New England's furious protest at President Jefferson's dismissal of Elizur Goodrich as Collector of the Port of New Haven had elicited but one sentence of comment from Whitney; to Stebbins he had written: "You have doubtless heard of the N Haven Remonstrance if you have not I have no time to tell you." The learned Dr. Smith, Denison Olmsted the naturalist, and the scientist Benjamin Silliman had seen in him greatness apart from his worldly accomplishments. His neighbor, the gifted Samuel Finley Breese Morse, had been happy to paint the portrait of that strong, intelligent face.

Testimony to the mark he had made upon New Haven — no one in that city of "steady habits" had been horrified at his unconcern for the future of his soul. Inspector Carrington had been right in observing Whitney's singular lack of interest in his hereafter. Although he had contributed to the New Brick Church in New Haven and attended services there, and although he had counted Timothy Dwight and other ministers of the Gospel among his good friends, he had remained at the end of his life, as in mid career, a stranger to religious emotion.

In a lesser man inattention to his salvation might have shocked his Puritan neighbors. Eli's brother Benjamin alone seems to have worried about it. In replying to a request from Henrietta for an account of her husband's boyhood, Benjamin, who had remained on the farm in Westborough, spoke from his Puritan stronghold. Informing the widow that he had nothing to tell of his brother's early life, he volunteered to discuss brother Eli's chances of future bliss.

By what I learned out of letters from N. Haven respecting what passed between yourself & him, who was your Husband and my Brother, in quite the last part of his life concerning his Eternal Interest, that it is not only possible but even probable that you have been an Instrument in the hands of God of making him a vessel of mercy.

Allowing this great object has failed, still your tender care to accomplish it calls for my highest Gratitude and Respect — That in addition to all your other kindnesses to him while connected in this life, you have not neglected, but carefully attended to that which *sums up the whole,* that which, if accomplished, will be a source of unspeakable joy to you; to me; to all his friends; yea to all the Angels in Heaven.

And now, dear Sister, let us work out our own Salvation in fear & trembling; knowing that it is God that works within us both to will & to do of his own good pleasure.

To these pious sentiments brother Eli would have perhaps paid lip service, but his entire life proclaimed his faith in himself to will and to do. For all his outward orthodoxy, his was a doctrine of self-help.

In a dozen ways, Whitney, while a product of his age, anticipated a later era. Without detracting from his magnificent courage and extraordinary intellectual grasp, students today may discern in his approach to the problem of his last illness an attitude of mind distinctively modern, perhaps distinctively American. Unable to tolerate doing nothing but wait, confident that, once he had assembled all the pertinent facts, he could accomplish something constructive, he turned to the invention of a mechanical device. Implicit in his thinking and action is the inner conviction that while prayer might help, something tangible, some mechanism, would be quicker and more certain. In the America of the Golden Day, the transcendentalists had not yet lost to the men of action. If, at Jefferson's death in 1826, justification by faith meant faith in a political system, science and invention nevertheless had not yet become the accepted means of justification by works. Whitney's life foreshadowed a time when new values would arise. His dedication to his work, his refusal to let death itself halt it, his absorbed interest in machines and in scientific principles, his very passion for efficiency, all are more characteristic of the modern world than of the United States in the early nineteenth century.

Gaps in his interests also set him apart from many men of his time. He excluded from his thoughts all matters not immediately relevant to the goals he set for himself. No comment whatsoever appears in his letters about the institution of slavery, although it was his gin that gave it new life. He seemed to take that social system for granted. Yet he must occasionally have seen, if he noticed at all, uncomfortable sights on Southern plantations or in the slave markets of Savannah or Washington. In 1819 and 1820, reports of the heated debates over the Missouri Compromise must have echoed in his ears, but somehow he failed to hear. He waved aside all political discussion, save when he was directly affected. When he learned that Congress in 1818 was proposing to raise the custom duties on iron, as an importer of foreign iron he lost no time in writing to Senator David Daggett of Connecticut: "It may be laid down as a general rule that the state of advancement in agriculture is always in proportion to the excellence of the instruments of husbandry in general use

& that the implements used in cultivating the soil of any Country will always be found to be improved & multiplied in proportion to the facility and cheapness with which iron can be obtained." Though kindhearted, Whitney ignored the first stirrings of movements for organized charity. In literature, other than scientific treatises, he had no interest at all. Architecture may have caught his attention, since that art touched on engineering. Paintings, in his eyes, were apparently primarily a means of perpetuating for posterity a picture of oneself. His was a completely single-track mind — the only kind of mind, Woodrow Wilson once said, worth having at all.

To remark upon Whitney's sharply limited interests is not to belittle his far-reaching achievements. His concentration upon a narrow field of endeavor, in the exploration of which he tended to let impersonal problems submerge those of human relationships, shows him as the forerunner of the specialist of the business age. His was neither the Renaissance ideal of the fully rounded man nor that of the eighteenth-century philosophers who looked for human perfectibility. Whitney looked for the perfectibility of machines. Yet while he was concerned with tangible things, he was also concerned with the physical laws that guided the mechanical production of things. In that sense, he was pledged to scientific research.

The twentieth century distinguishes between basic and applied research, the former aimed solely at widening the boundaries of human knowledge, the latter directed at putting that knowledge to use. Newton at the end of the seventeenth century opened the gates to an understanding of the physical world through which students of the *Principia* passed into a realm where the eighteenth century could put scientific principles to work in solving acute economic problems. Then, as later, a few men straddled the delicate line between pure and applied research to make contributions to both. In America, for example, Benjamin Franklin's experiments revealed new truths about the nature of electricity, and his practical application of his discovery produced the lightning rod. Whitney was not one of that small group of men who successfully combined both kinds of endeavor. His work was entirely practical.

Americans today would call Whitney a mechanical engineer. But at a time when engines were a novelty in the workaday world, engineering — the very term scarcely known — was an unrecognized profession. Trained men laboring to resolve everyday difficulties through use of the laws of mechanics were a rarity in Europe as well as in America. Schools qualified to teach the sciences essential to rapid technical progress had not yet come into being. The true innovator had to find for himself all but the most elementary data, unless, unlike Whitney, he had associations with men whose findings could supplement his. Circumstance tended to drive him into research whether he would or no. Individuals, such as Simeon and Selah North in the course of manufacturing pistols, now and again hit upon ways of improving their product and of saving hours of labor. Their procedures, however, grew out of purely empirical knowledge, whereas Whitney's derived also from theory. The firm foundation he thus laid for his work added to its solidity.

Whitney, possessed of the best scientific education eighteenth-century America could offer, was exceptionally well fitted to direct technological advances in a new and undeveloped country. Ambitious and resourceful, he took a path that led him to fortune. If chance first introduced him into the little explored field of invention and manufacturing, deliberate choice based on examination of his gifts and his country's needs later kept him there. His chosen profession called for utmost use of his book learning and his native talents. Caught by his vision, through his intellectual insights and his manual dexterity he was able to give his ideas visible working form. The world of primitive tools into which he was born had become at his death a world with an endless potential for prosperity.

From Whitney's concepts and the work of his hands came the Cotton Kingdom of the South and the industrialism of the North. The inventor of the cotton gin was certainly not the sole inventor of the "uniformity system," but it gained its original momentum in the manufactory at Mill Rock. There, while men elsewhere were developing new features of the plan, the Blake brothers kept the method alive in musket manufacture until in the 1840's Eli Whitney, Junior, was ready to take over. During the forties and fifties the Connecticut clockmakers, the producers of Elias Howe's sewing machine, the precision instrument makers of Rhode Island and, above all, the arms makers popularized and refined the processes of manufacture by machine. Yet it is scarcely asserting too much to say that the two aspects of Whitney's pioneering work at the opening of the century met in conflict on the battlefields of the Civil War.

Long before then, however, men had all but forgotten what Whitney's name stood for. In the South, the gin had become such a familiar tool that even cotton growers lost sight of its origin. In 1832, only seven years after Whitney's death, a South Carolinian felt impelled to publish an article about the inventor, in order, the author said, to rescue from oblivion the name of the great benefactor of the South. That brief publicity had little immediate effect. Not until the end of the century did school textbooks begin to include the simple notation: "In 1793 Eli Whitney invented the cotton gin." In the North, the very speed with which industrialists followed his lead helped obliterate the memory of what his pioneering work had meant. Since he took out no patents on the machine tools he invented, and since he never built his machines for sale, his name was not attached to his most important innovations. Tool builders of a later generation consequently did not realize what they owed to him. After 1822, for example, no one spoke of the milling machine as the Whitney miller, though gunsmiths talked of the stocking lathe as the Blanchard lathe and their descendants would call newer machines by the name of the companies introducing them. To this ignoring of Whitney's special place in American industrial history his son inadvertently contributed. Eli Whitney, Junior, though an able manufacturer, failed to maintain the pace his father had set in adding to his factory year after year new machines of his own design; hence the younger man had no special prestige in the burgeoning machine tool industry, and its leaders came to think of the Whitney Armory as merely another arms factory, instead of the birthplace of much of the interchangeable system. Finally, because technological history is still very new, the achievements of the gifted pioneer are only now beginning to receive the recognition they deserve.

After the Civil War, cotton grown under a new labor system for years again ruled in the South, but, with the passing of the decades, machines and machine tools have come to dominate the life of the entire United States. Americans are traditionally the great improvisers, and other men besides Whitney early in the nineteenth century were perceiving how to overcome the handicap the lack of labor imposed. This man, nevertheless, who relied upon self-help, whose faith in himself marked his career from start to finish, carried further than any single contemporary the new industrial order. His fame should rest more securely upon that accomplishment than upon the cotton gin itself. For the initiation of the mass production that has given the United States the highest material standard of living of any country in the world, the nation is indebted to the genius of Eli Whitney.

A Note on the Sources

THE SINGLE most important source of information about Eli Whitney is the collection of his papers housed in the Yale University Library. They include a considerable body of correspondence, books of Miller & Whitney, and some of Whitney's accounts. These materials, assembled by Henrietta Edwards Whitney after her husband's death, must form the backbone of any biography of the inventor. Second in value only to these are the official records of the War Department located in Washington, D.C., at the National Archives. Here lies most of the material dealing with Whitney's Government contracts and directly related matters. Supplementary to these two major manuscript collections are the Blake family papers, Ezra Stiles's "Literary Diary," and the Baldwin Collection, all in the Yale University Library; the Jefferson and the Madison papers in the Manuscript Division of the Library of Congress; in Boston the Massachusetts Historical Society's collections of Jefferson correspondence — microfilm of which is in the Library of Congress; the Oliver Wolcott papers in the possession of the Connecticut Historical Society; and Whitney's will and the inventory of his estate in the Connecticut State Library in Hartford. The three volumes of circuit court records of Georgia, 1793 to 1816, are in Savannah in the Record Room of the Superior Court, Chatham County.

Writings of Whitney's contemporaries, published in part or

in full, are also illuminating. All that survives of the text of Justice William Johnson's decision on the cotton gin rights, as the judge gave it in the circuit court in Georgia in December 1806, is to be found in *Federal Cases, Circuit and District Courts, 1789-1880,* Vol. 29, pp. 1070-72, No. 17,583. *The Papers of Thomas Jefferson,* edited by Julian P. Boyd, contain in Volume 8 (Princeton, N.J., 1953) a letter written to John Jay on 30 August 1785 describing Leblanc's work. The report of the Napoleonic officer H. Cotty, *Mémoire sur la Fabrication des Armes Portatives de Guerre,* explaining French difficulties in using Leblanc's methods, is in the Bibliothèque du Musée de l'Armée in the Hôtel des Invalides in Paris. Denison Olmsted, *Memoir of Eli Whitney, Esq.,* published in 1846, includes an essay by Benjamin Silliman and information brought together earlier from the recollections of several other men who had known Whitney well. Memoirs and biographies of men of the period and reports and studies of American problems eke out the picture of Whitney's time.

On individuals and public affairs:

American State Papers, Class III, *Finance.* Vols. I-III, 1789-1822; Class V, *Military Affairs,* Vols. I and II, 1789-1825. Washington, D.C., 1832-1834.

GIBBS, GEORGE: *Memoir of the Administration of Washington and John Adams,* ed. from the papers of Oliver Wolcott, Secretary of the Treasury. 2 vols. New York, 1846.

GOODRICH, S. G.: *Recollections of a Lifetime.* 2 vols. New York, 1856.

SMITH, MARGARET BAYARD: *The First Forty Years of Washington Society,* ed. Gaillard Hunt. New York, 1906.

WANSEY, HENRY: *An Excursion to the United States of North America in the September of 1794.* Salisbury, England, 1798.

On the New England scene and Yale College:

BALDWIN, EBENEZER: *Annals of Yale College.* New Haven, 1831.

BARBER, JOHN W.: *Historical Collections of Connecticut.* New Haven, 1838.

DWIGHT, TIMOTHY: *Travels in New England and New York.* 4 vols. Edinburgh, 1823.

HOLMES, ABIEL: *The Life of Ezra Stiles.* Boston, 1798.

KENDALL, EDWARD A.: *Travels Through the Northern Parts of the United States in the Years 1807 and 1808.* 3 vols. New York, 1809.

SILLIMAN, BENJAMIN: *An Address Delivered Before the Association of the Alumni of Yale College in New Haven, August 17, 1842.* New Haven, 1842.

WHITNEY, ELI: *Oration on the Death of Mr. Robert Grant, Member of the Senior Class . . . Aetat. XXIII.* New Haven, 1792.

On the South, cotton and the cotton gin:

BAINES, EDWARD, Jr.: *History of Cotton Manufacture in Great Britain.* London, 1835.

COXE, TENCH: *Memoir of Feb. 1817 (and of Dec. 1818) upon the Cotton Wool Cultivation, the Cotton Trade, and the Cotton Manufactures of the United States.* Philadelphia, 1817-1818.

HAMMOND, M. B.: "Correspondence of Eli Whitney Relative to the Invention of the Cotton Gin," *American Historical Review,* Vol. III, No. 1, October, 1897.

JOHNSTON, EDITH D.: "The Kollock Letters, 1799-1850," *Georgia Historical Quarterly,* Vol. XXX, September and December, 1946.

MELISH, JOHN: *Travels Through the United States of America in the Years 1806 and 1807, and 1809, 1810, and 1811.* London, England, 1818.

RAMSAY, DAVID: *History of South Carolina.* 2 vols. Charleston, S.C., 1809.

SCARBOROUGH, WILLIAM, "Sketch of the Life of the Late Eli Whitney with Some Remarks on the Invention of the Saw Gin," *Southern Agriculturalist,* Vol. V, No. 8, August, 1832.

WHITE, GEORGE S.: *Memoir of Samuel Slater, the Father of American Manufactures.* Philadelphia, 1836.

To this list three works dating from mid-century should perhaps be added:

CAIRNS, J. E.: *The Slave-Power.* New York, 1862.

DeBow, J. D. B.: *The Industrial Resources of the Southern and Western States.* 3 vols. New Orleans, 1852-1853.

OLMSTED, FREDERICK LAW: *A Journey in the Seaboard Slave States with Remarks on their Economy.* New York, 1856.

On American science and invention in general:

American Journal of Science, more especially of minerology, geology and other branches of natural history; including also agriculture and the ornamental as well as useful arts. Conducted by Benj. Silliman, M.D. 2nd ed., Vol. I. New York, 1819-1846.

EVANS, OLIVER: *The Young Millwright and Miller's Guide.* 4th ed. Philadelphia, 1821.

UNITED STATES PATENT OFFICE: *List of Patents Granted by the United States, April 10, 1790 to December 31, 1836.* Washington, D.C., 1872.

On firearms and interchangeable manufacture:

BENÉT, STEPHEN V. (ed.): *A Collection of Annual Reports and Other Important Papers, Relating to the Ordnance Department, Taken from the Records of the Office of the Chief of Ordnance, from Public Documents and from Other Sources.* 4 vols. Washington, D.C., 1878-1890.

HICKS, JAMES E.: *Notes on United States Ordnance.* 2 vols., 1940.

A volume dealing with developments after Whitney's death s:

STEARNS, CHARLES: *The National Armories.* 2nd ed., Springfield, Mass., 1852.

Secondary sources, including special studies of the period, of particular problems, or of Whitney's part in solving them, are fairly numerous. The only complete and satisfactory biog-

raphy of the inventor is that of JEANNETTE MIRSKY AND ALLAN
NEVINS: *The World of Eli Whitney* (New York, 1952), a book
valuable at once for its insights and for its extensive quotations
from Whitney's letters and other contemporary sources.

For other biographical data and the general American scene,
see:

ADAMS, HENRY: *History of the United States* (1801-1817). 9
    vols. New York, 1921.

BARBER, JOHN W.: *History and Antiquities of New Haven.*
    New Haven, 1856.

BLAKE, WILLIAM P.: *History of the Town of Hamden, Con-
    necticut.* New Haven, 1888.

DEXTER, FRANKLIN B.: *Biographical Sketches of the Graduates
    of Yale College* (1701-1815). 6 vols. New York, 1885-1912.

Dictionary of American Biography, eds. Allen Johnson and
    Dumas Malone. 21 vols. New York, 1928-1937.

ELLET, ELIZABETH F.: *The Court Circles of the Republic.* Hart-
    ford, Conn., 1869.

FORBES, HARRIETTE M.: *The Hundredth Town, Glimpses of
    Life in Westborough, 1717-1817.* Boston, 1889.

FULLER, GRACE P.: *An Introduction to the History of Connec-
    ticut as a Manufacturing State.* Smith College Studies in
    History, Vol. I. Northampton, Mass., 1915.

GREEN, CONSTANCE McL.: *History of Naugatuck, Connecticut.*
    New Haven, 1948.

GREENE, GEORGE WASHINGTON: *The Life of Nathanael Greene.*
    3 vols. New York, 1867-1871.

HENDERSON, ARCHIBALD: *Washington's Southern Tour, 1791.*
    Cambridge, Mass., 1923.

HUTCHESON, HAROLD, *Tench Coxe: A Study in American Eco-
    nomic Development.* Johns Hopkins University Studies in
    Historical and Political Science, New Series, No. 26. Balti-
    more, 1938.

KROUT, JOHN A., AND FOX, DIXON RYAN: *The Completion of
    Independence, 1790-1830.* Vol. V, *A History of American
    Life.* New York, 1944.

MORGAN, DONALD G.: *Justice William Johnson, The First*

Dissenter, The Career and Constitutional Philosophy of a Jeffersonian Judge. Columbia, S.C., 1954.

PARSONS, FRANCIS: "Ezra Stiles of Yale," *New England Quarterly,* June, 1936.

———: *Six Men of Yale.* New Haven, 1939.

WEEDEN, WILLIAM B.: *Economic and Social History of New England, 1620-1789.* 2 vols. Boston, 1890.

For cotton, the gin and cotton manufacture:

BAGNALL, WILLIAM R.: *The Textile Industries of the United States.* Cambridge, Mass., 1893.

BATES, EDWARD C.: "The Story of the Cotton Gin," *New England Magazine,* new series, vol. 2, May, 1890.

DODD, WILLIAM E.: *The Cotton Kingdom.* New Haven, 1921.

HAMMOND, M. B.: *The Cotton Industry: An Essay in American Economic History.* Part I: "The Cotton Culture and the Cotton Trade." American Economic Association. New York, 1897.

LEWTON, F. L.: *Historical Notes on the Cotton Gin.* Smithsonian Report for 1937. Washington, D.C. (Publ. 3478).

PHILLIPS, ULRICH B.: *Life and Labor in the Old South.* Boston, 1929.

TOMPKINS, DANIEL A.: *The Cotton Gin: The History of its Invention.* Charlotte, N.C., 1901.

WARE, CAROLINE: *The Early New England Cotton Manufacture.* Boston, 1931.

WILLIAMS, ERIC: *Capitalism and Slavery.* Chapel Hill, N.C., 1944.

For American science and invention:

BATHE, GREVILLE AND DOROTHY: *Oliver Evans: A Chronicle of Early American Engineering.* Philadelphia, 1935.

BRASCH, F. E.: "The Royal Society of London and Its Influence upon Scientific Thought in the American Colonies," *Scientific Monthly,* XXXIII, 1931.

JAFFE, BERNARD: *Men of Science in America: The Role of Science in the Growth of Our Country.* New York, 1944.

KRAUS, M.: "Scientific Relations Between Europe and America

in the Eighteenth Century," *Scientific Monthly*, LV, 1942.

STRUIK, DIRK: *Yankee Science in the Making*. Boston, 1948.

UNITED STATES PATENT OFFICE: *Brief History of the United States Patent Office From its Foundation*, 1790-1886. Washington, D.C., 1886.

USHER, ABBOTT PAYSON: *A History of Mechanical Inventions*. New York, 1929.

WOLF, A.: *A History of Science, Technology, and Philosophy in the Eighteenth Century*. London, England, 1938.

For the history of precision manufacture and the development of firearms:

BRAMSON, ROY T.: *Highlights in the History of American Mass Production*. Detroit, 1945.

DEYRUP, FELICIA J.: *Arms Makers of the Connecticut Valley: A Regional Study of the Small Arms Industry, 1798-1870*. Smith College Studies in History, Vol. XXXIII. Northampton, Mass., 1948.

FITCH, CHARLES H.: *Report on Manufactures of Interchangeable Mechanism*. U.S. Census, 1880, Manufactures. Washington, D.C., 1883.

FULLER, CLAUD E.: *The Whitney Firearms*. Huntington, W. Va., 1946.

GREEN, CONSTANCE McL.: "Light Manufactures and the Beginnings of Precision Manufacture," *Growth of the American Economy*, ed. Harold F. Williamson. New York, 1946.

HARTE, C. R.: *Connecticut's Iron and Copper*. Annual Report Connecticut Society of Civil Engineers. New Haven, 1944.

HUBBARD, GUY: "Development of Machine Tools in New England," *American Machinist*, Feb. 14, 1924.

KEITH, H. C., and HARTE, C. R.: *The Early Iron Industry of Connecticut*. Reprinted from the 51st Annual Report of the Connecticut Society of Civil Engineers. New Haven, 1935.

NORTH, S. N. D. and RALPH H.: *Simeon North, First Official Pistol Maker of the United States*. Concord, N.H., 1913.

ROE, JOSEPH W.: *English and American Tool Builders*. New Haven, 1916.

————: *Connecticut Inventors.* Tercentenary Commission of the State of Connecticut. New Haven, 1934.

SAWYER, CHARLES W.: *Firearms in American History.* 3 vols. Boston, 1910.

SHARPE, PHILIP B.: *The Rifle in America.* 2nd ed. New York, 1947.

More general books:

BISHOP, J. LEANDER: *A History of American Manufactures, from 1608 to 1660.* 2 vols. Philadelphia, 1861-1864.

CALLENDER, GUY S.: *Selections from the Economic History of the United States* (1765-1860). Boston, 1909.

CLARK, VICTOR S.: *History of Manufactures in the United States.* 3 vols. New York, 1929.

COCHRAN, THOMAS C., and MILLER, WILLIAM: *The Age of Enterprise.* New York, 1942.

COULTER, ELLIS MERTON: *Georgia: a Short History.* Chapel Hill, N.C., 1947.

KEIR, ROBERT M.: *Manufacturing.* New York, 1928.

MCMASTER, JOHN B.: *A History of the People of the United States.* 8 vols. New York, 1883-1913.

MUMFORD, LEWIS: *The Golden Day: A Study in American Literature and Culture.* New York, 1934.

Acknowledgments

For assistance in the preparation of this book I owe a special debt of thanks to Jeannette Mirsky, author with Allan Nevins of the first life of Whitney to be based upon all his extant papers. Conversations and exchange of letters with her cleared away a number of my uncertainties. I am equally indebted to Felicia Johnson Deyrup, formerly my student at Smith College, now assistant professor at the New School in New York City, and to Irving B. Holley of Duke University. Miss Deyrup, whose familiarity with the problems of precision manufacture in Whitney's day is even wider than the knowledge embodied in her excellent monograph on the early arms industry in the Connecticut Valley, has generously shared her findings with me. Mr. Holley, author of the illuminating study *Ideas and Weapons*, contributed invaluable suggestions for handling difficult technological discussions and through his searching questions and comments helped me re-examine my every postulate and my every conclusion.

Since much of this book is the fruit of more than fifteen years' investigation of scattered materials dealing with New England industrial history, I dare not attempt to name all the individuals who have assisted me at one time or another. Custodians of private collections of papers and the staffs of public repositories alike have invariably been courteous and helpful. I wish to thank Mr. Stephen Riley, Librarian of the Massachusetts Historical Society, for allowing me to quote from Jefferson letters owned by the Society. My obligation is particularly deep to Mr. James T. Babb, Librarian of Yale University, for permission to use the library's manuscript collections, and to Mrs. Zara Powers, in charge of the Whitney papers, for aid in identifying obscure materials and in deciphering some nearly illegible passages. My son-in-law, Ronald Frazee, did me the inestimable service of locating in the Hôtel des Invalides in Paris the official report of 1806 on French interchangeable manufacture. My thanks also go to members of the staff of the National Archives and Library of Congress, most of all to Mr. Frederick Arnold, until recently a reference librarian at the Congressional Library, now in charge of serial publications at the Princeton University Library.

Finally, I wish to make grateful acknowledgment to my daughter and son-in-law, Lois Angell and Allen Reynolds Clark. Their critical judgments, born of careful study and understanding of the period, have sharpened my perceptions of its quality, just as their sense of literary style inspired in me constant effort to tell a dramatic story simply.

Index